1-11-2012

To Columbia College with best wishes to all the criminal justice majors.

Mark S. Schneider
Deputy Warden Missouri State
Penitentiary (ret.)
Columbia College MSCJ-2001

Shanks to Shakers: Reflections of the Missouri State Penitentiary

Mark S. Schreiber

Copyright © 2011 by Mark S. Schreiber and
Jefferson City Convention and Visitors Bureau
100 E. High Street, Jefferson City, Missouri 65101

Shanks to Shakers
Layout and typesetting: Sarah Alsager
Printer and binder: Walsworth Publishing Company, Inc.
ISBN: 978-0-615-50378-3

All rights reserved. Printed and bound in the United States of America.

15 14 13 12 11 5 4 3 2 1

Dedicated to:

Bill M. Armontrout,
a mentor who for 40 years has stood by me in good times and bad.

Fr. Clarence Patrick Wheeler,
who taught me to temper authority with compassion.

John A. Viessman,
who taught me the priceless value of our rich Missouri heritage.

the staff of the Missouri State Penitentiary/Jefferson City Correctional Center,
who, in 2011, observe their 175th anniversary,
and
the employees of the Missouri Department of Corrections.

Preface	
Photographs	**Page 1**
Postcards	**Page 45**
Staff-Related Items	**Page 59**
Restraint and Locking Devices	**Page 71**
Contraband: Dangerous	**Page 81**
Contraband: Nuisance	**Page 101**
Art: Paintings to Carvings	**Page 117**
Miscellaneous Artifacts	**Page 135**
Acknowledgments	**Page 147**

HOLLOW WALLS

Silence falls upon this place where thousands walked, cried, embraced.

Near two centuries have now elapsed since these walls were first encapped.

I hear the shuffle of their feet.

In silence each is in retreat along these hollow walls.

Their sunken cheeks, the vacant stares as each goes by without a care

beside these hollow walls.

Ten thousand souls have seen this place,

have shrieked aloud, their souls encased within these hollow walls.

Now, as I prepare to leave, their ghosts remain with no reprieve

within these hollow walls.

Shuffle, shuffle, hear their feet in silent lockstep they repeat.

Chains dangle from their feet as hammers ring the dead man's beat

within these walls, forever.

Mark S. Schreiber
01.03.2002

We Americans are a nation of collectors. If more than two items relating to the same subject can be located, we label it a collection. Countless books ranging across an endless spectrum have been written on collections. There have been publications on police and fire collectibles. There are museums dedicated to police and fire services, and there are a few good prison museums. Thousands of books specifically relate to prisons or corrections. But books addressing prison artifacts are rare. Perhaps we don't wish to recognize beyond certain social boundaries that there are artifacts from prisons that are part of our social history. Like it or not, such items should be preserved.

Prisons played a unique and significant role in the development of nineteenth- and early twentieth-century industry in America. In many cases prisons were an industry. Missouri was a classic example. Operating for well over 100 years under the Auburn, Lease, and Contract Labor systems, the Missouri State Penitentiary (MSP) at various times operated a stone quarry, brickyard, lumberyard, tannery, wagon-making shop, multiple boot and shoe factories, twine plant, broom factory, clothing factories, furniture factory, metal plant, and the largest saddletree factory in the world.

This publication is not intended to be an inclusive history on corrections and prison artifacts, for such an undertaking would be impossible. My purpose in creating this book is to specifically address some artifacts related to the history of the old Missouri State Penitentiary in Jefferson City, Missouri. Tucked away in attics, basements, garages, antique shops, and flea markets across Missouri, and no doubt beyond, are thousands of artifacts from the old MSP. In my 42 years of working with staff and inmates who served at the prison, I have come across numerous unique items. Many were illegally made and seized as contraband. Others are unique and beautiful works of art. All are pieces of Americana. From the earliest days of my association with the prison, I recognized that such items were significant and should be retained.

I also know that over the years, through the administrations of numerous wardens and other state officials, more was thrown away than was kept. Prison ledgers, books, reports, glass-plate photo images, furniture, artwork, and miscellaneous items were taken to the prison dump. Some were destroyed by fires and in disturbances that occurred over a period of 168 years. Many times I have been asked, "Where did you acquire such a collection of so many artifacts?" Collecting becomes compulsive. One item leads to more. The high comes from the hunt, and the hunt never ends.

My quest began when I found my first weapon in the ball dugout at Ozark Stadium located inside the MSP. It was a knife well made from a stainless-steel shop ruler. The markings were clearly visible. Black electrical tape was wrapped around one end to make a handle. The edges were filed razor sharp, and one end had a needle-sharp point. When I asked shift Captain Leroy Casey what he wanted me to do with the weapon, he told me to get it out of the prison. "Take it out, throw it away, or keep it," I was told. From that day on I was hooked on the artifacts and history of the old prison. During the 1970s and 1980s hundreds of weapons and other contraband items were removed from MSP. Items involved in actual crimes had to be secured as evidence. None of my collection of artifacts was used as evidence. Items that were recovered in common areas or could not be linked directly to an inmate were removed by staff and disposed of or kept.

A large segment of my collection was obtained because other individuals knew of my interest in prison artifacts and history. The late Warden Harold R. Swenson; Richard Nash, deceased son of late Warden E. V. Nash; John Eidson, son of the late Warden Ralph Eidson; the late Warden Donald Wyrick; retired Warden Bill Armontrout; and many others helped me in my search for MSP history. I spent a small fortune purchasing artifacts, usually one or two at a time, from former staff members and other individuals. Antique shops, flea markets, and local yard and estate sales have been good sources. Several years ago a local antique dealer showed me what was thought to be a leather cane. I told him the item was a line stick that staff used to direct inmate movement. What was a twenty-dollar item became a hundred-dollar item!

While in Springfield, Missouri, some years ago, I found several original MSP documents in a well-known military collectibles store. The documents were written during the administration of MSP Warden Horace

Swift (1865–1869). I paid only a few dollars for them. That store would have been the last place I would have expected to find prison documents.

Collectors should beware when purchasing items alleged to have come from any specific prison, especially if the item is a shackle or other restraining device. Locks, handcuffs, and ball-and-chain devices are often sold as being from a notorious prison. Use caution! Most early items were not marked with a prison name. This certainly applies to articles from MSP. Recently I was contacted by a lady who asked me to stop by her house as she had something for me. She gave me an oak stick that her father had carried in the main dining room at MSP during the 1954 riot. The item is a piece of her history and ours. When I was the special investigator for Cole County Prosecuting Attorney James F. McHenry, I acquired a number of MSP items. None had been used as evidence in a court case.

Among the most historically valuable items are photographs. The late Louis "Mickey" Bredeman, long-time Cole County court reporter, related to me his personal experiences regarding the prison. He gave me numerous photographs of the 1954 riot. Jefferson City attorney Edgar Eagan was secretary of the prison Bipartisan Advisory Board during the 1930s and gave me a number of photographs of MSP. Many others have contributed to my collection through the years. I took many photographs during my positions as an investigator and prison administrator and kept my photos. Sometimes the one item or subject that might seem the least significant, initially, has the greatest historical significance later. Keep your photographs and label them!

Talk to people and let them share their stories. The late Cole County Circuit Judge James T. Riley told me many stories about his prison involvement when he was Cole County prosecutor. Numerous prison employees, law officers, offenders, and their family members have shared their MSP experiences. Once individuals discover your interest, they will often donate or allow you to photograph their items. Some items that I located would have been great additions to my collection, but they were overpriced. Once-abundant items may be quite rare today. I had been searching for tobacco made at MSP. It proved to be more elusive than I had anticipated. I was taken by surprise when Mr. and Mrs. Bob Van Ark asked me if I had any tobacco made at the prison. I was astounded when they presented to me a small pouch of prison-made tobacco. The cloth pouch still had the lettering on it and the cigarette papers attached to the side. You never know!

I wish to make one clarification in regard to the writing of this book. It was not my intention to write about myself. It was my intention to relate some social history through my personal experiences and relationships with MSP staff and offenders. I relate this in my own words as I witnessed it. Each individual who worked behind the walls of MSP

Moving day, September 15, 2004. *Mark S. Schreiber photo.*

has a personal history. Their stories should be told, recorded, and preserved. We often don't think of ourselves as being part of history. History isn't just the major events that capture the headlines. For the most part, history consists of small everyday slices of life, whatever they may be. My greatest regret is that I did not keep a diary. A few entries each day would have been sufficient. I wrote hundreds of reports on everything from homicides to escapes. Regretfully, few copies have survived. Once a case or investigation was closed, files were purged by those who came after me, and historical documentation was lost.

When the old prison was closed in 2004, several file cabinets containing original classification cards were transferred to the Missouri State Archives. Shortly before I retired from the Missouri Department of Corrections in 2010, I received information that thousands of old MSP identification photographs, additional classification cards, and entry ledgers were in danger from rodents, insect damage, and environmental conditions. Staff at the Fulton Reception and Diagnostic Center fortunately recognized the historical significance of the old MSP records in storage there. With their assistance we were able to transfer 76 boxes of photographs and other material to the Missouri State Archives.

Some will read this book from front to back; others will skip randomly through it, examining items of interest to them. Readers may find information repeated when it is intertwined with more than one topic or artifact. It is hoped that this book is enjoyable, informational, and will serve to increase awareness of the history of the old Missouri State Penitentiary and of our own individual historical significance; provide a resource for the student of corrections history; encourage volunteer participation in assisting men and women who are incarcerated in prisons; and encourage incarcerated offenders to explore and develop their talents so they may return to society as productive citizens. If any of these objectives can be fully or partially accomplished, this publication will have served its purpose.

View from a cell in Housing Unit 4/A Hall. *Mark S. Schreiber photo.*

History: The Fortress on the Hill

At one time the Missouri State Penitentiary was hailed as the "greatest in the world." Thousands of men and women lived, worked and died behind its high stone walls and beneath the long shadows of sixteen watch towers. Many thousands were imprisoned there, others were employed there; all are a part of the prison's long history. Like a Gothic fortress, the penitentiary loomed on limestone bluffs high above the Missouri River. Its collection of 52 buildings resembled a giant puzzle. The entire prison property was 142 acres— 105 acres existed outside the wall, 37 inside. On September 15, 2004, after having been in existence almost 100 years before the famed Alcatraz Federal Prison, the Missouri State Penitentiary in Jefferson City closed its doors after 168 years of operation. It was the oldest continuously operating penitentiary west of the Mississippi River.

The year was 1831 when Governor John Miller, Missouri's fourth elected governor and the first to hold office in the City of Jefferson, requested that the Missouri General Assembly build a prison in the city. Only a village at that time, the City of Jefferson was located in almost the geographic center of the state, east to west. After much debate, on January 3, 1833, the House approved a bill to establish a penitentiary with a vote of 25–24. The Senate passed the bill with an 11–6 vote. Daniel Dunklin was then Governor of Missouri.

Philadelphia architect John Haviland is believed to have designed the first prison building, and James Dunnica, who constructed the first State House in the City of Jefferson, was the Superintendent and Commissioner of Construction. The first building on the site was constructed of limestone quarried on the prison site. The design called for 40 cells, the dimensions of each to be 8' by 14'. There was to be a total of three cell blocks, a warden's house and a wall of stone. The first cell block was completed in 1835. On February 29, 1836, during the time of the Siege of the Alamo in Texas, the Missouri State Penitentiary received the first inmate, Wilson Eidson of Greene County, Missouri. As the prison population grew, convict labor was used to construct additional buildings as needed through the years.

Initially, the prison operated under the Pennsylvania System that did not condone the use of corporal punishment but concentrated on reforming the convict's soul. Inmates were confined in a solitary environment where each could reflect on his sins. This system failed in the eastern prisons, where it was initiated under the influence of the Quakers, and it also failed in the Missouri Penitentiary. As a result, the Auburn System, named for the Auburn Prison in New York, became the standard for over 30 state prisons including Missouri where it was used for over 100 years. Under this system inmates were confined in separate cells at night but were allowed to work together during the day. The rule of silence was strictly enforced, and inmates could not speak to each other without permission. To do so would result in harsh punishment that would be initiated for the smallest infraction. Along with the Auburn System came cat-o-nine tails, rings, lockstep and the water torture. Convicts were clothed in zebra-striped uniforms purposely made of coarse material to make the individual as miserable as possible.

From the 1870s until after the turn of the 20th century, the MSP influenced the industrial expansion of the City of Jefferson. Inside the prison were multiple shoe and boot factories that produced up to 10,000 pairs of shoes and boots every two weeks. The J. S. Sullivan Saddle Tree Factory was the largest manufacturer of saddle trees in the world, making in excess of 60,000 annually. As labor unions became organized across the U.S., the Missouri State Penitentiary became a "poster child" as to why in a free industrial market convict labor should not be used in competition with union labor. Some of the first millionaires in Jefferson City made their fortunes within the walls of MSP and built their mansions just outside the walls.

From a population of 14 inmates in 1836, MSP grew to be one of the largest prisons in the United States with a population of around 5,000 in 1932. Among the cast of offenders who did time behind the walls were: George Thompson, seminarian, abolitionist, author; General John McDonald, soldier, politician, author; John Reno, former soldier, train robber; J. B. "Firebug" Johnson, thief, arsonist, robber; the Young brothers,

Paul, Jennings, and Harry, small-time thieves turned cop killers; Harry Snodgrass, armed robber who became known as "King of the Ivories;" Charles Arthur "Pretty Boy" Floyd, small-time hood, armed robber, Most Wanted; Lee Sheldon- aka "Stagger Lee," St. Louis waterfront worker, killer and music ballad legend; Adam Ricchetti, small -time hood, member of Floyd's gang, executed at MSP; Fred Hildebrand, fall-partner with Floyd; Emma Goldman, outspoken social reformer, radical socialist; Kate Richards O'Hare, social reformer, antiwar activist, author; Mattie Howard, Kansas City underworld "darling", killer, author, self-proclaimed religious leader; Charles "Sonny" Liston, poor St. Louis youth, armed robber, boxing champion; Carl Austin Hall, alcoholic, small-time crook, kidnapper/killer; Bonnie Brown Heady, prostitute, alcoholic, girlfriend to Hall, kidnapper/killer; James Earl Ray, thief, robber, escapee, killer.

The MSP became known as an extremely violent prison; its reputation was well-documented. In the 1960s a national publication referred to it as the "bloodiest 47 acres in America." The "bloody" reference was accurate, but the walls of MSP contained only 37 acres. Persons have questioned how a prison could be so violent. From 1836 until 1989 it was the only maximum-security prison operated by the State of Missouri. There was no other place to house "the worst of the worst."

Even though the MSP employees and staff were among the lowest-paid prison workers in the nation, they were concerned about violence in the prison. One tragic incident occurred at the door of Housing Unit 5/J & K Hall one May evening in 1969, when inmate Roger Harling was approached by inmate Ronald Westberg. Westberg had a psychopathic personality and was known to be unpredictable and dangerous. He walked up to Harling and without warning produced a knife and began to stab him. Harling ran out of the door, down several steps with Westberg in pursuit. Harling's screams could be heard as he reached the steps near the main dining room and Housing Unit 4/A Hall. As he ran up the steps, Westberg caught him again and stabbed him. At the top of the steps near the front of Housing Unit 4/A Hall, Harling ran toward the Captain's Office. Westberg continued his assault. In front of the Captain's Office, Roger Harling collapsed and fell into a flower bed. Westberg struck the fatal blow, unconcerned if anyone saw him. An older officer walked over to where Harling lay, looked down at him and fainted. When he regained his senses, the officer walked out of MSP and never came back. Ronald Westberg later hanged himself. This was the first of many acts of violence that I became involved with through the years.

That same year Officer James Eberle and I stood watch all night by the bedside of Officer Patrick Cayce after he had been severely stabbed by a berserk inmate in the metal plant. He was so severely injured that Jefferson City surgeon Dr. Stuart Exon directed that he not be removed from the MSP hospital until he recovered enough to be transferred to another hospital. Ironically, Officer Cayce's life was saved by inmate Red Dolan. A former U.S. Navy Corpsman, Dolan was a surgical assistant to Dr. Exon and Dr. L.E. Giffen as they performed medical procedures at the MSP hospital.

On January 20, 1975, the body of Lt. Harold Atkinson was found stuffed under a bunk in Cell #296, Housing Unit 2/F & G Hall. He had been stabbed 69 times. The brutal death of a well-liked officer shocked MSP to its core. I was on the lead team to investigate his murder. Four years later I investigated the murder of Officer Walter Farrow who was stabbed in the chest with a knife that had been taken from a cabinet in the vegetable preparation room. Clinton Wyrick, another MSP employee, nearly lost his life in the same incident but used his feet to ward off the attacker.

These are examples of how violence can erupt without warning and death can occur from the use of handmade contraband weapons created surreptitiously by clever minds. Capable investigators who solved hundreds of cases associated with MSP include Arthur W. Dearixon, Sam Morris, George Brooks, Pat Mantle, Richard Lee, David Spicer, John C. Hemeyer, George Payne, Roy Fluegel, Don Wells and Bud Shipley. Cole County Sheriff Wyman S. Basinger was always there to help when a situation became difficult.

The photos and narration in this book are an historical overview of life at the old Missouri State Penitentiary portraying tragic, humorous, sentimental and routine, but never boring, events that occurred within the stone walls. Captain John Motel said it best when he gave the last official MSP radio transmission on September 15, 2004: "One hundred and sixty-eight years of tradition has ended. A new tradition now begins."

I was fortunate to have served with the courageous and capable men and women who, in our time, illuminated the Missouri State Penitentiary.

Mark S. Schreiber

Cell 10, Death Row Housing Unit 3/C Hall, 1988. In 1989, all of the men on death row were moved to the Potosi Correctional Center at Mineral Point, Missouri. Missouri became one of two states that mainstreamed inmates with a capital punishment sentence into the general prison population. Mark S. Schreiber photo.

Prisons, in every aspect, have always lured photographers. On the following pages are some of the thousands of photographic images taken of the old Missouri State Penitentiary during its 168-year history. Rarely does a week go by that some previously undiscovered image does not surface. No doubt, there are hundreds of photographs of MSP that remain hidden in attics, basements, trunks, scrapbooks, boxes, and drawers. Unfortunately, many have been thrown away or destroyed. As these images are viewed, perhaps others, long forgotten will be retrieved to take their place for all to enjoy as a part of the MSP story and our Missouri heritage.

Photographs

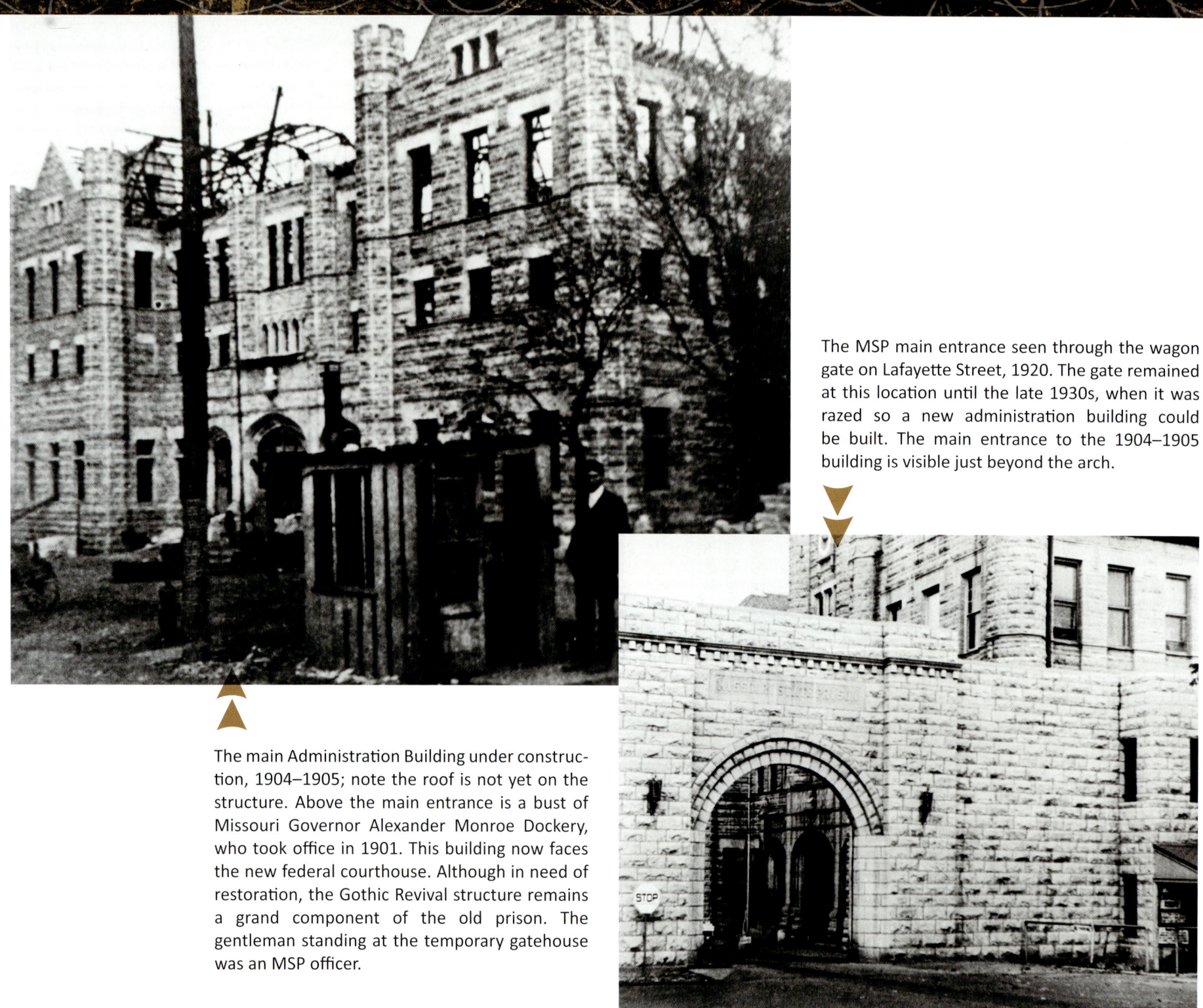

The MSP main entrance seen through the wagon gate on Lafayette Street, 1920. The gate remained at this location until the late 1930s, when it was razed so a new administration building could be built. The main entrance to the 1904–1905 building is visible just beyond the arch.

The main Administration Building under construction, 1904–1905; note the roof is not yet on the structure. Above the main entrance is a bust of Missouri Governor Alexander Monroe Dockery, who took office in 1901. This building now faces the new federal courthouse. Although in need of restoration, the Gothic Revival structure remains a grand component of the old prison. The gentleman standing at the temporary gatehouse was an MSP officer.

The third-floor Food Service in the D Dorm, 1937. The building sat next to Housing Unit 3/B & C Hall.

Final preparations for the hanging of Edward Raymond, George Ryan, and Harry Vaughan, who shot their way out of MSP on November 24, 1905, resulting in the deaths of three staff members. A fourth inmate, Hiram Blake, was shot and killed by authorities during the escape. The three men were captured and tried and were hanged, side-by-side, on June 27, 1907, at the site of the old Cole County Jail. The June 27, 1907, *Cole County Democrat* ran the headline "Jerked to Eternity." The historic jail was razed, and the Jefferson City Police Department is now on the site.

In 2009, the author was giving a presentation in Jefferson City when he was approached by John Sullivan Jr., whose family the author had known for 50 years. John presented the author with ten original photographs that his father had taken. John stated that the photos depicted MSP in the 1920s, when the elder Sullivan had been a corrections officer. A few years later he joined the Jefferson City Fire Department and served as its chief for many years.

John Sullivan Jr. said that he had no idea what the photos of MSP showed. Examination by the author revealed that the photos were remarkable, as they were of Housing Unit 4/A Hall when the roof had burned off in the winter of 1927. Over 700 inmates had to sleep in the outside courtyard in the sleet while the roof was being repaired. This photo shows the inmates and staff around the entrance to Housing Unit 4/A Hall removing debris from the roof fire. Old E Hall is visible behind Housing Unit 4/A Hall. Snapshots of this sort are historically valuable; they should be labeled and never thrown away.

This photo was taken May 1, 1916, by Jefferson City photographer T. G. Cooper. The dark building in the background was Centennial Hall, circa 1848. It was later torn down, and a portion of it remains buried. In the foreground, Punishment Hall inmates are tearing down a structure to make way for what would be the west wing of Housing Unit 3/B & C Hall (McClung Hall). This hall was named for MSP Warden D. C. McClung. To the left in the photo is the completed east wing. Of interest in the photo are the mules and wagons.

These convicts are marching from the old D Dorm dining hall, 1908, in single file and lockstep, which was a part of the Auburn System. Housing Unit 4/A Hall is at the left, and an officer is on the walk at lower center.

An unknown photographer took this great photo of the Missouri State Penitentiary Band, circa 1920.

The MSP Concert Band, circa 1920.

▲ The upper lawn, previously called the courtyard, circa 1970. Housing Unit 4/A Hall is at left. The flower beds were well maintained, and the reflecting pool remained until the construction of the chapel in the 1980s. The remains of the old dining hall were torn down following the destruction of the building by fire in the 1954 riot. *Mark S. Schreiber photo.*

▲ The MSP courtyard in the 1920s. Housing Unit 4/A Hall is to the left with a prison shop behind it. The old dining hall is at the right. Note the inmates and staff by the dining hall entrance. Note also the courtyard pool. *Sullivan collection photo.*

Another view of the courtyard, taken about 1936. To the left is Housing Unit 4/A Hall, which, at the time, was an African-American unit. Housing Unit 3/C Hall is in the background, and the captain's (yardmaster's) office and deputy warden's office are in the building at right. The photo was taken from the north, looking south. *Eagan collection photo.*

The main courtyard at MSP in 1930. The gate at left is part of the Administration Building. Note the spittoon by the stone step. The white door at center reads: "Deputy Warden's Office." Housing Unit 4/A Hall is at right, and old E Hall is behind Housing Unit 4/A Hall. *Eagan collection photo, given to Schreiber.*

The old visiting room at MSP prior to the one that was completed around 1938. *Eagan collection photo.*

These MSP officers are dressed in their summer uniforms, circa 1930. Some are carrying line sticks or batons. Today, none of these white uniforms or hats are known to exist.

This cabinet-style photograph was taken during the administration of Warden J. M. Sanders. Tom M. Scott was the deputy warden and later warden from July 26, 1939, to July 17, 1941. The officers in this photo are wearing their summer uniforms. Sanders and Scott are at top right. Regrettably, each officer cannot be identified in this historic photo.

Staff and inmate laborers stopped construction work on the gas chamber building to pose for this photograph in 1937. The chamber was delivered to the MSP site, and portions, including the vent stack, were assembled. The stone building that included two holding cells and a witness area was then built around the chamber. The prison wall is in the background. Frank Marshall is at right wearing a hat and dark suit. The MSP officer at right, wearing the old-style blue suit and officer's cap, is unidentified. He carries a billy club in his right hand. The inmates are unidentified. This photo was donated to the author in 2008 by H. D. Marshall.

An MSP Engineering Department staff member observes renovation of the gas chamber building in 1988. To prepare for the execution of George "Tiny" Mercer the chamber, which had not been used since 1965, required several repairs. A new vent stack, seen at the center of the photo in the middle of the roof, replaced the old metal stack pipe that had rusted out. The roof was sealed, interior painting was done, and seating for witnesses was constructed.

To the right of the walk is a gurney that was obtained from the Missouri State Surplus Property Agency. It was placed inside the chamber, which is located through the door on the right. The steel chairs that had been used for lethal gas executions were removed and stored. Later they were placed back inside the chamber. *Mark S. Schreiber photo.*

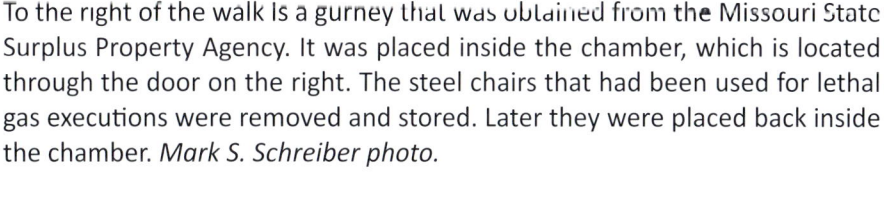

The gas chamber under construction, 1937. The photo proves that inmate labor was used to build the structure. Inmate workers are seen at left and right. This photograph and several others were received in 2008 from H.D. Marshall, whose father, W. F. (Frank) Marshall, is shown wearing a suit and hat. Frank was the construction supervisor at MSP during the 1930s.

The window in the gas chamber building was removed in 1988 and made into a door to be used as an entrance for persons witnessing the execution of George "Tiny" Mercer. Unlike the late 1930s, when the gas chamber was first used, in the late 1980s some witnesses had to be in separate rooms. Note the top of the steel gas chamber can be seen behind the winch used to lift the blocks of stone.

The gas chamber building as it appeared a few years following its construction in 1937. Condemned inmates were driven from death row, located in Housing Unit 3/B & C Hall, to the gas chamber location. The death house contained two holding cells, where the condemned were kept for a short time prior to execution.

Two examples of card-style invitation passes issued for specific executions at MSP. They were issued to individuals selected by the warden to be witnesses to executions conducted in the gas chamber. Passes were not issued for all executions. Four colors for the passes are known to have been used. They were pale green (in frame) pink (at left), blue and yellow.

The gas chamber was used a total of 39 times, beginning in 1938 and ending in 1965 with the execution of Lloyd Leo Anderson. This photo was taken by the author in 1988 as the gas chamber was being prepared for the execution of George "Tiny" Mercer. Because of concern that the chamber might leak, a Missouri statute was changed to allow lethal injection to be the method of execution. Mercer was executed by injection in January 1989.

The chairs seen in this photo were removed and replaced with a gurney. Mercer was the first and last person to be executed by lethal injection at MSP. Warden Bill M. Armontrout was in charge of the execution. Following this execution, all men on death row at MSP were transferred to the new Potosi Correctional Center at Mineral Point, Missouri.

A view of the gas chamber inside the stone structure which houses it. The lever at lower right was pulled to release the cyanide tablets into a container inside the chamber. The wheel-type devices on each side of the gas chamber door had to be turned at equal rates to seal the door; failure to do so would result in the cyanide gas leaking from the chamber and endangering the staff who were just outside the door.

The lever at upper right was pulled following an execution to open a vent that went from the chamber to the outside. The fan on top of the chamber was activated to pull the gas outside. Clearing the chamber took from 45 minutes to an hour, and then the chamber door could be opened.

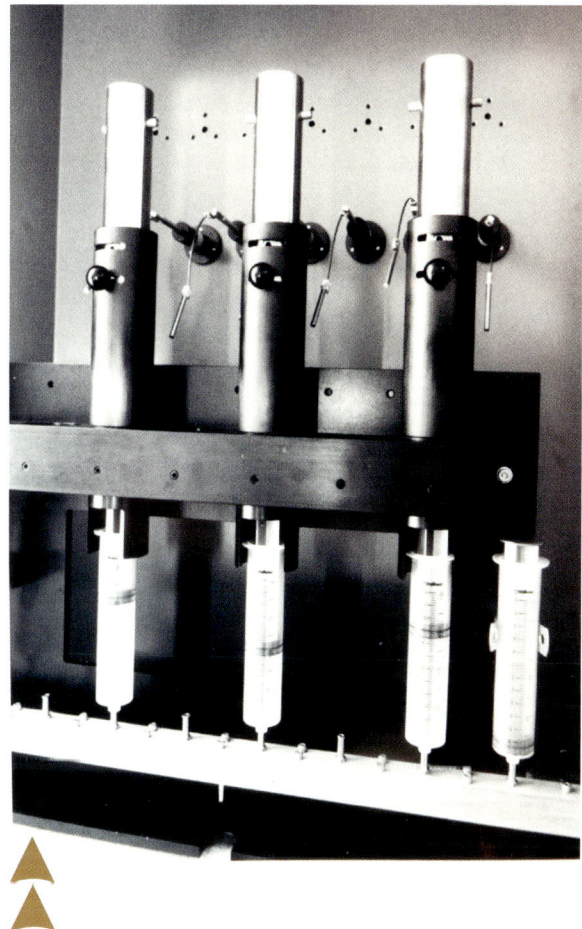

The interior of the lethal injection machine once used by the State of Missouri is seen in this photo. The machine was used for only a few executions as there were too many problems with this device. Missouri switched to an IV system for lethal injection executions. *Mark S. Schreiber photos.*

The visitors' entrance located at the corner of Lafayette Street, with the main perimeter wall at right, circa 1920. Currently, this is the east side of the intersection at State and Lafayette streets. Visitors wishing to tour a portion of the prison or who were visiting an inmate entered this door. The sign reads: "Visiting on Saturdays, Sundays, and Holidays from 9:00 A.M. until 2:00 P.M." The lower sign reads: "Notice: Anyone desiring to enter prison either on business or pleasure will be required to submit to being searched. Order of Penal Board."

Two MSP officers are shown at the old main entrance ready to escort a visitor into MSP, circa 1937. *Eagan collection photo, given to Schreiber.*

Nine empty barber chairs await inmate customers in this 1953 photo of the central clothing and shower area. The chairs were from the Koken Barber Company, St. Louis, Missouri. The last of these antique chairs was removed from MSP about 1980.

Three photos unite to complete a panoramic view of MSP looking west. The date is probably in the late 1950s. First, a number of buildings constructed in the 1930s, including the diesel power plant in the foreground, are completed. Second, old E Hall, second building to the left of the smokestack, is still standing. It was torn down in the 1960s. Third, buildings that were burned during the 1954 riot are no longer present. Last, the towers around the perimeter wall are mostly the old turret style, which remained until 1957–1961. This photo was given to the author by the late William Rutledge, who served as chief engineer and later as deputy warden at MSP.

An inmate crew works at the main prison garage and receiving entrance, circa 1950. Art Deco lights are on pillars; each light weighed about 300 pounds. The center pillar was removed later as vehicles became too large to go through either side. The gate top and sides and the lights were saved when the area was cleared for the new federal courthouse, which is now located on the site.

Well-known Hollywood gangster actor Wallace Beery is shown with an unidentified young lady in this photo taken by Jefferson City news photographer Bob Blosser. Beery came to MSP to check on his one-time chauffeur who was serving time. *Bob Blosser photo.*

This October 19, 1938, view was taken from the southwest and is looking east rather than south. Several newly constructed PWA and WPA buildings are shown: the hospital at center background, the garage at left foreground, and the administration building at upper right. All of these structures were taken down after the prison was closed in 2004. A new federal courthouse stands on approximately 7.5 acres of the site. *Eagan collection photo, given to Schreiber.*

The new MSP hospital and tuberculosis dorm, February 15, 1939. The project was completed on October 1, 1938, at a cost of $436,000. *Eagan collection photo, given to Schreiber.*

Night scene of MSP with the Missouri State Capitol at center background, circa 1950. The prison was a far different and more eerie world when night came and the institution was wrapped in shadows.

View from the MSP water tower located east of the prison, 1977. MSP officials Warden Donald Wyrick, Deputy Wardens Bill Armontrout and Calvin Beard, Chief Engineer Bill Rutledge (later deputy warden), Superintendant I Urban Lock, Captain Leroy Casey (later colonel), and the author often met at the water tower to discuss serious issues regarding the prison. The group became known as the "Water Tower Gang." At night MSP was a different world, dark and lonely with fog frequently rolling in from the Missouri River, which bounded the prison on the north. There were hundreds of places to hide inside the 52 buildings and the mile of tunnels that ran under the huge complex. In this photograph the corner of Housing Unit 3/B & C Hall is at left. Housing Unit 1/H Hall is in the center and Housing Unit 4/A Hall is at right. Barely seen above Housing Unit 4/A Hall is the prison hospital. Gate 2 is at the middle foreground, and the M&M building is the low building at right center. Most of the prison cannot be seen from this viewpoint.

The 1954 MSP riot as observed from the 700 block of East Capitol Avenue. Flames roar unchecked from factory buildings located inside the walls. The fires were seen in the night sky from 30–40 miles away. No fire units could enter the prison because the inmates were not contained and could escape through the gates. Missouri Highway Patrol units raced to the prison from across the state, their vehicles ruined from overheated engines. *Joe Kroeger photo.*

John D. Eidson is seen at far right holding an original Thompson submachine gun, one of three owned by the prison. Eidson was 17 when the photo was taken. His father, Ralph N. Eidson, was warden when the riot erupted at MSP on September 22, 1954, the date this photo was taken.

John told the author that he was at home in the warden's residence, 722 East Capitol Avenue, directly across from the south perimeter wall, when the riot occurred. Warden Eidson was fishing at the Church Prison Farm (Central Missouri Correctional Center) located on the old Boonville Road (Highway 179). John drove out to the prison farm and told his father that a riot had started. His father told him to make certain that all of the trustees assigned to the warden's house were locked up in L Hall, which was outside the main prison compound. Eidson remembers that the trustees were very nervous and concerned about going back to L Hall, but they followed instructions. Warden Eidson soon returned to MSP and found it in flames.

The woman in the photo is the first female UPI reporter in the area, Jerena East Giffen. She had previously covered the execution of Bonnie Brown Heady and Carl Austin Hall in 1953. The three Thompson submachine guns are still in the prison armory. *Tom E. Tetrick photo, courtesy of John D. Eidson.*

Aerial view of the massive fires that swept the night during the riot. The inmates did not burn the housing units; however, a number of support buildings and industry structures were burned, resulting in a loss in the millions of dollars. *St. Louis Post-Dispatch photo.*

Mist from the Missouri River and smoke from the fires shroud the Missouri State Penitentiary the morning after the riot. Most of the burned buildings were out of range in this aerial shot, taken by a *St. Louis Post-Dispatch* photographer. At the time of the riot, the author was in the third grade and recalls seeing and hearing planes circle overhead all the next day. Several burned factories were located just beyond Housing Unit 2/F & G, at top left. Other burned buildings are down the hill at the extreme left. The building at upper left appears to be attached to the large, castlelike Housing Unit 3/B & C Hall. The exterior walls are black from the fire that raged in the library and education sections. Holes can be seen where the roof burned. *St. Louis Post-Dispatch photo.*

The shell of old E Hall awaits the wrecking ball, 1967. Windows and bars from the 1880s structure are already removed. The infamous 1954 riot started at 6:45 p.m. on September 22, on the top floor of this building.

Following the 1954 riot several inmates were charged as ringleaders and the killers of inmate Walter Lee Donnell. Here, the ringleaders are being escorted into Cole County Circuit Court by members of the Missouri State Highway Patrol. From left to right: Donald De Lapp, age 19; William "Billy" Hoover, age 23; Jack L. Noble, age 19; Rollie Laster, age 21; Paul Kenton, age unknown, and James "Slick" Stidham, age 28. Wearing a suit and seated is Col. Hugh Waggoner, superintendent of the highway patrol. Other troopers pictured are Capt. Maurice Parker (center left), Lt. Bill Barton (center right), and Sgt. Jim Judkins (upper left).

Walter Lee Donnell was killed in the segregation unit because he was a "snitch" and was hated. He snitched on a number of individuals, including Irv Thompson and Richard Lindner, who were members of an organized St. Louis armed-robbery gang. Donnell was being held in death row segregation for his own protection. Previous attempts on his life had been made in St. Louis.

Another hated inmate was James Creighton, age 51, who was serving life. Creighton burned one convict to death by throwing gasoline in his cell and had slashed the throat of another inmate. Attempts to kill Creighton during the riot failed because he blocked his cell door track with trash and jammed the lock to the cell.

Donnell and Creighton were in the last two cells in death row (south side of Housing Unit 3), where the cells remain today. The inmates wanting to kill Creighton obtained a broomstick, tied a knife to it, and attempted to stab him through the cell bars. Creighton avoided death but did receive an injury to his jaw. He was later released from MSP because the state could not protect him. It is unknown what happened to him.

Inmate Sammy N. Reese had come to MSP as a young teenager when given the death penalty for two murders, and was also on death row at the time of the riot. He saw men enter the death-row unit during the riot and heard the murder of Donnell. Reese told the author in 1970 that an inmate named Thompson killed Donnell, presumably Irv Thompson. Warden Donald Wyrick told the author he knew that Thompson had killed Donnell. Several of the men charged for their activity in the riot were sentenced to die in the gas chamber, but none were executed. Sammy Reese, the author's art student, had his death sentence commuted to life, got out of MSP on parole, and died of natural causes. The author knew Jack L. Noble well and talked with him in later years. Noble said that he was involved in starting the riot but had killed no one. He admitted that he hated "Slick" Stidham and would like to see him dead. Noble was a very rough character.

Following the conviction of the ringleaders, there was much speculation as to their guilt. A former MSP inmate-turned-feature-writer for the *Kansas City Star*, J. J. Maloney, wrote an article that brought out a number of issues regarding the conviction of the ringleaders. Maloney's article was based on an alleged deathbed confession made by former inmate Irv Thompson around 1981, when he admitted to his sister that he had killed Walter Lee Donnell. He added that should he (Thompson) die, his sister should let the authorities know the truth. She related the information to Warden Donald Wyrick. Maloney was a talented writer but liked to "stir things up" while an inmate at MSP. As to who killed Donnell, questions remain today. *Zeal Wright photo.*

Missouri Corrections director Thomas Whitecotton (light suit), Missouri State Highway Patrol Major E. I. (Mike) Hockaday (center right), and MSP Warden Ralph N. Eidson (glasses) discuss strategy during the 1954 MSP riot. *Missouri State Patrol photo.*

Roundup of inmates on September 23, 1954, following a night of rioting. Note the burned out truck and the stretcher with an outline of a body in blood. *Sid Pohlman photo.*

MSP reconstruction in 1956–1957. Inmate labor was used to rebuild several of the buildings, including this building that served as the library, school and dining hall during its existence. It was gutted by fire during the 1954 prison riot. Housing Unit 3/B & C Hall is visible in the background.

Inmates reconstruct the maintenance building which was burned during the 1954 riot. The corner of Housing Unit 4/A Hall is at far left. The brick building at left is Housing Unit 5/J & K Hall. The smokestack at center was part of the old prison power plant.

Through the years, several celebrities visited MSP, including, in later years, Barbara Mandrell, Willie Nelson, Johnny Paycheck, and Archie Moore. Sonny Liston learned to box behind the walls and returned to visit with inmates and staff. Here, world-champion boxer Joe Louis visits with MSP champ Jeff Meritt and Sandy Saddler, middleweight champ. Louis is at right and Saddler is at left.

This panoramic view of the baseball field inside the MSP walls was taken in 1933. Looking southwest, the old prison rock quarry is in the middle background. *Cresswell of Kansas City photo.*

MSP baseball team, circa 1964. Jerry James, second from right, back row, is the only team member identified here. Teams from the Jefferson City area often came to the prison to play the MSP team. This photo was taken on the lower yard (Ozark Stadium) with the wall behind the team. The photo was given to the author by Ed Hanauer Jr., an employee at MSP.

In about 1920, Jefferson City photographer Carl Deeg took this photo of the MSP baseball team posed on the upper lawn, with Housing Unit 4/A Hall in the background. The old-style windows were changed around 1940.

A Little League baseball team plays in MSP's Ozark Stadium in the 1960s. Many such teams played at MSP until the practice was stopped for security reasons. At one point, the prison sponsored a local Little League team called the Fledglings, coached by MSP Lt. Edward Hill.

MSP inmates enjoy the great American pastime in Ozark Stadium, circa 1965. The original old wall is in the background. Housing Unit 5/J & K Hall is visible at middle background. *Ed Hanauer Jr. photo.*

Major League ballplayers visit MSP, sometime after 1938 (Housing Unit 2/F & G Hall, in the center background, is completed). The names of the ballplayers unfortunately have been lost. The inmates seated on what was once a stone quarry were no doubt elated to have professional players visit inside the walls. Note the men crowded directly behind the sports heroes.

Warden Harold R. Swenson stands in the upper yard of MSP, June 1967. The photographer was Roy Cook of the *St. Louis Globe-Democrat*.

MSP tactical E-Squad members conduct a major search of Housing Unit 4/A Hall, April 13, 1992. Teams conducted searches in an orderly manner. Prior to entering cells, inmates were frisked to make certain contraband was not concealed on their person.

Searching is a vital process to the successful management of a correctional facility. Equally important is the manner in which it is done. Every effort should be made to not unnecessarily damage or destroy inmate personal property. *Mark S. Schreiber photo.*

The interior of Housing Unit 4/A Hall photographed in 1930 before new cell doors were installed. The very short doors were part of the harsh Auburn System that was embraced by Missouri Corrections for over 100 years.

MSP staff and members of the tactical E-Squad unit line the upper walks of Housing Unit 4/A Hall during a major search on April 13, 1992. Contraband furniture and other items that were removed from cells strew the main floor, called "the flag" in prison slang.

Fifteen large dump truck loads of contraband furniture were removed. The material had accumulated over a period of several years. It was necessary to remove the items because they caused difficulty in conducting searches and were also a fire hazard. The search was code named Operation Spring Cleaning. *Mark S. Schreiber photo.*

Three inmates shoot the breeze in front of the captain's office, circa 1980. At left is inmate Larry D. Winjen, #19330, who died in MSP. The middle inmate is J. D. Cox. The inmate at right is Mickey Shields, who coached boxing. He looked like a character straight out of a *Rocky* movie. Winjen caused a number of problems in the institution and was the first inmate the author had an encounter with in the Administration Segregation Unit. The large pile of dirt in the right background was the excavation site for the new prison chapel.

Three MSP men play miniature golf in the upper yard near tower 3. The golf course was the idea of Department of Corrections Director Fred Wilkinson, who attempted to improve conditions at the prison during the late 1960s and early 1970s. Wilkinson was no "bleeding heart" by any means. He had the reputation of being tough, but fair. The miniature golf course was a good idea; however, its existence soon came to an end when an inmate was assaulted and killed by another inmate using a golf club as a weapon.

The main prison lower yard as it appeared on July 4, 1958. Mrs. E. V. Nash, wife of the late Warden Nash, gave this photo to the author.

Inmate Stevens sits on his bucket near the captain's office in the 1970s. Like many older, long-term inmates, he became a favorite of the offender population and the staff. Older inmates were elevated to a certain status. Stevens sat on his bucket when not doing his garden work. When Stevens died, Warden Bill Armontrout had a flower wreath placed by the man's bucket.

Former Department of Corrections Director Fred Wilkinson (center) and MSP Warden Wyrick (right) near Housing Unit 6/D Dorm. The MSP hospital is behind them. Wilkinson was a well-known and respected federal prison warden before he became the director of the Missouri DOC, a position he held from 1965 to 1972.

Inmate journalist Lou Miller, a very intelligent man whom the author knew well, views the gas chamber shown at middle right in this 1960s photograph. The large open space at right is the prison ball field. The 1930s powerhouse is the building in the background, middle. The building at upper left, above Miller's head, was the women's prison, which was in use until 1960. From 1842 until 1926, women inmates were housed behind the walls of the main prison.

Inmates pose on the roller-skating rink, circa 1973. The author investigated an assault at MSP where two inmates were chasing each other with knives while roller-skating. One suffered serious stab wounds.

A typical inmate cell, located in Housing Unit 3/B & C Hall, circa 1970. The cardboard at lower left was placed on the bars to reduce the draft. Sometimes blankets were hung for the same purpose. Neither was allowed because of security issues and the potential fire hazard.

Inmate Jack L. Noble in his cell in Housing Unit 4/A Hall in 1981. He came to MSP as a very young man and was later charged as a ringleader in the 1954 MSP riot. Eventually he was paroled, but he violated it and returned to the Department of Corrections.

The interior of Noble's cell is ornate, complete with a 90 gallon aquarium, swivel desk chair, curtains, mirror, and a walnut dresser made of contraband wood from the MSP furniture factory.

The practice of allowing inmates in certain units to have well-furnished cells was not uncommon. Early postcard images from the 1920s show fancy cells. The practice had to be suspended because of the extreme fire danger, especially in Housing Unit 4/A Hall, where there was only one point of exit. *Mark S. Schreiber photo.*

Interior of Housing Unit 4/A Hall, 1981. Pool tables were placed on the main floor of the housing unit. They later had to be removed because the inmates began using pool cues and balls as weapons. *Mark S. Schreiber photo.*

An interior view of Housing Unit 3/C Hall (McClung Hall), circa 1930. Note how the windows opened to provide air circulation.

Inmate laundry is draped over the rails outside of cells on upper-level walks of Housing Unit 4/A Hall. Although hanging laundry over the rails was discouraged, it was recognized by staff that most inmates wanted to maintain personal hygiene. *Mark S. Schreiber photo.*

Aerial view, looking northwest, circa 1990.

Only the shell of old I Hall remains at MSP. It was only used from the 1920s to 1946. I Hall's steel was removed for salvage. Bars would have existed along each walk where the support beams are located. The roof of old I Hall was reinforced concrete. Called the "Supermax of its day," the unit was constructed during the gangster era, when St. Louis and Kansas City gangs were making headlines. This unit was built to withstand the force of a dynamite blast. *Stephen Brooks photo.*

The top of the doorway to cell 46 is unearthed. Today, the cells of old Centennial Hall remain buried beneath an exercise area constructed for men in the death-row unit. *Mark S. Schreiber photo.*

In the 1980s, construction between Housing Units 2 and 3 provided an opportunity to explore the long-buried Centennial Hall, built around 1848. The old cell block had been razed years before, and the bottom part had been covered with dirt. When uncovered, the interiors of the cells were found to be dry. Several handmade iron straps used to hold the wooden doors were still intact.

Above at left, officials from the Division of Adult Institutions, the Department of Corrections, and the Missouri State Penitentiary examine the unearthed old cell block. From foreground to background: R. Dale Riley (in suit), Arthur Dearixon, George Lombardi (in dark suit), Major James Eberle (in uniform), Donald Cline (in suit, hands on hips), Captain Gary Blank (in uniform), Larry Henson (in tie, facing forward), and Sam Morris. The officer standing above is unidentified. *Mark S. Schreiber photo.*

A fallen steel door is all that remains as a reminder of conditions in the dungeon cells of Housing Unit 4/A Hall. A wooden door was closed over the steel-barred door to keep out light, air, and sound. Prisoners who were being punished could be placed in the total darkness of a dungeon cell by themselves or with other inmates. A "honey bucket" placed in one corner served as a toilet. Prisoners slept on the cold stone floor and received one meal per day that usually consisted of a cup of water and a piece of cornbread. Many went insane, died of disease, or committed suicide. The last use of the dungeon cells was in the late 1930s.

Aerial view looking northeast toward the Missouri River and the Callaway river bottoms, circa 1980. It was taken by Harvey L. Harris, a civilian photographer for the Missouri State Highway Patrol.

A unique view of the old prison, as seen from a location on Chestnut Street. Some of the prison cannot be seen, yet its emptiness is apparent. The parking lot at left was created after the prison was emptied. It was built over the prison baseball field. *Stephen Brooks photo.*

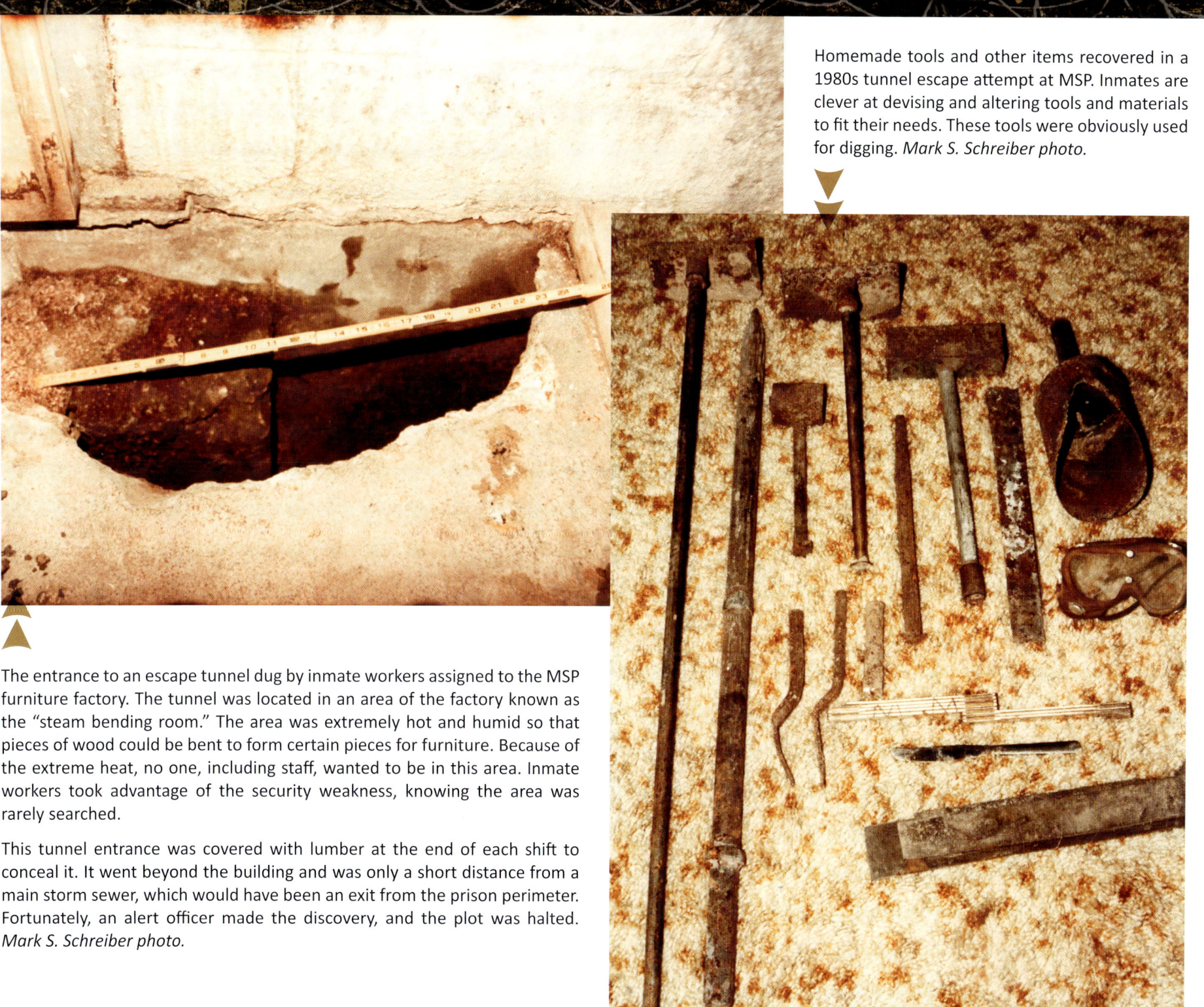

Homemade tools and other items recovered in a 1980s tunnel escape attempt at MSP. Inmates are clever at devising and altering tools and materials to fit their needs. These tools were obviously used for digging. *Mark S. Schreiber photo.*

The entrance to an escape tunnel dug by inmate workers assigned to the MSP furniture factory. The tunnel was located in an area of the factory known as the "steam bending room." The area was extremely hot and humid so that pieces of wood could be bent to form certain pieces for furniture. Because of the extreme heat, no one, including staff, wanted to be in this area. Inmate workers took advantage of the security weakness, knowing the area was rarely searched.

This tunnel entrance was covered with lumber at the end of each shift to conceal it. It went beyond the building and was only a short distance from a main storm sewer, which would have been an exit from the prison perimeter. Fortunately, an alert officer made the discovery, and the plot was halted. *Mark S. Schreiber photo.*

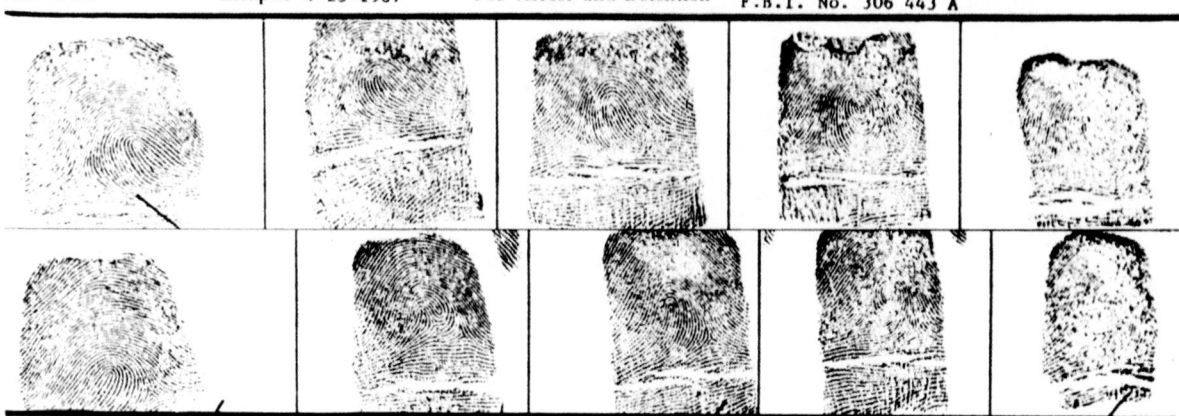

James Earl Ray was received at MSP on March 17, 1960, from St. Louis, Missouri, for auto theft and armed robbery. He received a 20-year sentence. His prison number was 00416. On April 23, 1967, Ray escaped from MSP by hiding in a large bread box from the prison bakery. He rode out of the prison in a prison delivery truck. The original reward for Ray was fifty dollars as shown on this wanted poster.

Following his escape from MSP, Ray dropped from sight until almost one year later. On Thursday, April 4, 1968, James Earl Ray was in a rented room in a boarding house in Memphis, Tennessee. From his window he took careful aim with a Remington Gamemaster 760 .30-06-caliber rifle and fired a single round at a man standing on the balcony of room 306 at the Lorraine Motel across the street. His shot struck the man, killing him almost instantly, changing the course of American history. Martin Luther King Jr., American civil rights leader, was dead as a result of Ray's vicious act.

Ray was taken into custody in London, England, in July. He was eventually sentenced to a term of 99 years, which he served inside the Brushy Mountain Penitentiary in Tennessee. While there, he attempted to escape twice. He was successful in breaching the perimeter once, but tracking dogs found him nearly frozen to death under a pile of leaves. In 1991, Ray was transferred to the River Bend Maximum Security Institution in Nashville, where he remained until his death in 1998. The Missouri Department of Corrections maintained an escape warrant for James Earl Ray until his death.

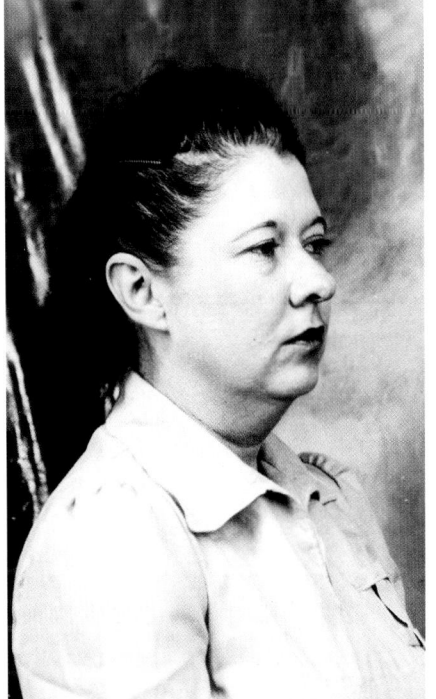
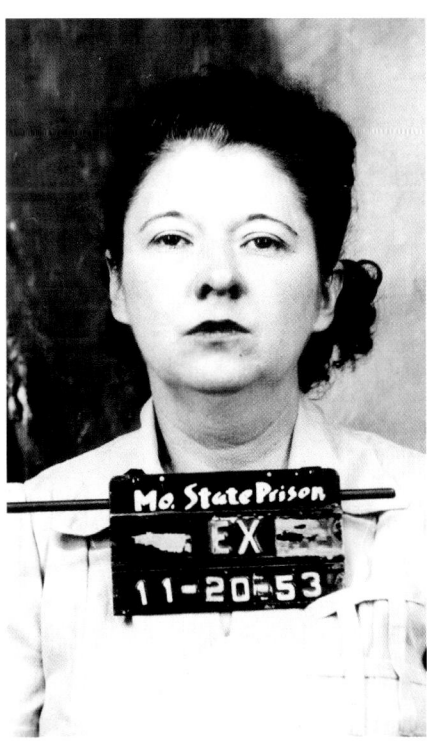

The official MSP photograph of Carl Austin Hall who, with his girlfriend, Bonnie Brown Heady (shown below), kidnapped and murdered 6-year-old Bobby Greenlease in 1953. Bobby's father, Robert Greenlease, was a multi-millionaire automobile dealer from Kansas City, Missouri.

Hall and Heady posed as Bobby's aunt and uncle. Heady went to the private Catholic school that Bobby attended and told the nuns that Bobby's mother was seriously ill. The unsuspecting nuns allowed Bobby to go with Heady. The couple attempted to strangle Bobby, but failed. They then shot Bobby to death, placed his body in Heady's vehicle, and drove to her residence in St. Joseph. His remains were buried in Heady's backyard.

Thinking their son was alive, the Greenlease family paid the $600,000 demanded in the ransom note. It was the highest ransom amount ever paid in the United States up to that time. After receiving the money, Hall and Heady went from St. Joseph to St. Louis where they freely spent the money. Authorities caught up with them at a St. Louis motel, the Coral Court. A portion of the ransom was recovered; however, almost half was missing and remains so to this day. It is believed that two St. Louis police authorities took a portion of the money.

The kidnapping of Bobby Greenlease received national attention. Hall and Heady were convicted of the crime and sentenced to die in the MSP gas chamber December 18, 1953, at 12:01 A.M. Warden Ralph N. Eidson executed them. They sat side by side at the end. Heady was the only female to be executed in the gas chamber.

Major B. J. Poiry and Warden Ralph Eidson stated to the author that Hall showed remorse for what he had done. Heady, however, showed no emotion or remorse. *Missouri Department of Corrections photos.*

Reporters race from the MSP garage to the nearest telephone following the execution of Carl Austin Hall and Bonnie Brown Heady on December 18, 1953. Phones were not provided, and reporters competed to get their story over the wire first. Photographer Bob Blosser captured the drama in this photograph.

Official photograph of Charles "Sonny" Liston, inmate 63723. He came to MSP on June 2, 1950, after being convicted with two other men for robbing a service station, cab stand, and café on Market Street in St. Louis. He was illiterate and one of 17 children.

At MSP he found his niche in life with the help of several staff, including Major B. J. Poiry. He learned to box and became a sensation. When a publisher of a St. Louis newspaper saw him in action, he contacted the Missouri Board of Probation and Parole and spoke with Parole Officer Richard Wiles. As a result, Liston was released from MSP in October 1952, and the newspaper publisher saw to it that Sonny had a job.

In 1953 Liston won the National Heavyweight Championship in Chicago. In the 1960s he returned to MSP to visit with staff and inmates. While incarcerated, Liston lived in Housing Unit 4/A Hall, cell 33. *Missouri Department of Corrections photo.*

Inmate 29078 was received at MSP on December 18, 1925. His name was Charles Arthur Floyd, known as "Pretty Boy." Little is known of Floyd's "fall partner" Fred Hildebrand, who came to MSP with him for a St. Louis, Missouri, payroll robbery. Hildebrand escaped the following year and was captured.

Floyd caused little trouble while at MSP and was released on March 7, 1929. This is his original prison photograph. *Missouri Department of Corrections photo.*

On the inside of the main perimeter wall bordering East Capitol Avenue, this fading image reigns high above what was once the MSP athletic field. This image of Sonny Liston, an MSP icon, was painted on the wall by inmate artist Isaiah Jackson. Where once a thousand men stood and cheered as Liston boxed, now a parking lot exists below his portrait. *Stephen Brooks photo.*

This block of stone with a small cross carved into it can be seen on the main perimeter wall, along Chestnut Street on the east side of MSP. Below the cross is the name "Cooper." The reason and purpose of this carving is unknown. Most inmates buried in the old prison graveyard had no tombstones. It remains one of the mysteries of MSP. *Stephen Brooks photo.*

A crosshatch steel door in Housing Unit 4/A Hall. This heavy handmade door could tell a thousand stories of punishment, pain, and suffering. It is an artifact from the period when the Auburn System ruled at MSP. The cell entrance height is around five feet. A prisoner had to bend each time he entered or left the cell. This practice and the zebra-striped uniform, the silent system, the lockstep, and the cat-o-nine-tails reminded the prisoners that they were nothing. All the cell doors on the property were as short as the one seen here, until the 1930s, when the doors were changed, reflecting a more humane direction in correctional philosophy. *Stephen Brooks photo.*

Construction on the MSP Administration Building was taking place when this photo was made. This is an example of Gothic Revival architecture. The stack of loose rock on the perimeter wall at left is to prevent inmates from attempting escape. A potential escapee trying to climb the wall would pull the loose rocks down, hitting himself. The postcard was printed in Germany for Manchester's Book Store, Jefferson City.

Advancements in photography and in the mass production of images enabled Americans to imagine travel beyond the confining boundaries of their everyday lives during the late 19th and early 20th centuries. The penny postcard came into its own. Every drugstore, newsstand, and hotel lobby sold penny images depicting America. People of all ages collected and pasted postcards into scrapbooks, notebooks, and albums. What would stir the imagination more than to send back home a postcard view of the Missouri State Penitentiary, hailed as "the greatest in the world"? The following pages contain a variety of postcard images of the old MSP. Equally as fascinating as the photos were the comments written on them. Postcards, like those who mailed them, have become forgotten fragments of our American heritage, lost somewhere in time just as someday each of us shall be.

Postcards

A wide-angle view of old MSP in an early 1900s Gilbert postcard. The photo was taken from the east.

A "Phostint" Card (9530) printed by the Detroit Publishing Co., circa 1910. Note the tower officer standing on the perimeter wall. A second staff person is at the base of the tower near the door. The old prison hospital is the red brick building at left.

The main entrance to the original Administration Building. Evidence of construction is visible by the board ramp on the steps leading to a boarded-up entrance with makeshift doorway. Note the ornate gate in the center opening. Outlines for hinges that held the gate can still be seen in the stone today. It is not known when the gate was removed or what happened to it.

The men in the photograph are wearing the style of clothing and hats of MSP officers in the early 1900s. The round circle above the center gate is a postmark dated September 8, 1906. This postcard bears no indication of photographer or publisher.

DINING ROOM STATE PENITENTIARY, JEFFERSON CITY, MO.

Many collectors prefer postcards that are in perfect condition; however, used cards are often more interesting as they reveal more information relating to dates. This postcard of the MSP dining room is dated July 4, 1909. Notice the plates are unlike the ones shown in the photo below.

The old MSP dining hall as it appeared circa 1909, with plates and tin cups on the tables. Published by Sam'l H. Smith & Co., Jefferson City, Missouri, postcard 12790.

12790 Dining Hall, Missouri State Penitentiary, Jefferson City, Mo.

A view of MSP looking west, dated January 2, 1908. In the foreground are the quarry operation and outbuildings on the prison property. The main perimeter wall runs across the scene. The present wall was not built at that time. The smokestack is from the prison's coal-fired power plant. At the extreme right background is the dome of the state capitol that was destroyed by fire in 1911. Postcard 3881, published by Sam'l H. Smith & Co., Jefferson City, (120566), a Litho-chrome postcard printed in Germany.

This view of MSP is almost identical to the Sam'l H. Smith postcard seen at right. When examined closely this view is different in several ways. The title is in the upper right corner. The post card is numbered 12801. The view here shows a different foreground; the sky is different. The most noticeable difference is the smoke; it is black in this view and is blowing north to south. In the similar photo the smoke is light grey and is moving in the opposite direction.

The Alfred S. Cote Publishing Co. of Jefferson City printed this panorama of MSP (postcard 7050).

B, C and E Halls, circa 1909. A new Housing Unit 3/B & C Hall was constructed circa 1914 and was called McClung Hall. The red brick building in the background is, allegedly, the old E Hall. This card may be misidentified since E Hall, built in the 1880s, was next to Housing Unit 4/A Hall. Postcard 12798 published by Sam'l Smith & Co.

An early 1900s photo of the MSP courtyard and the dining hall that was burned in the 1954 riot. A greenhouse is at right; Housing Unit 4/A Hall is at left. A new, larger dining hall was built circa 1938. Published by Sam'l H. Smith & Co., postcard 12797.

One of the most popular postcards from MSP was card 12795, showing convicts coming from dinner in 1908. Inmates are wearing striped clothing. Housing Unit 4/A Hall is seen at left. This is another Sam'l H. Smith postcard.

The Administration Building, foreground, and prison hospital. Many postcards are nearly identical except for slight differences in the wording or the angle of the image. E. C. Kropp Company, Milwaukee, 3208, postcard dated 1922.

A 1909–1910 view of the old warden's residence at 700 East Main Street (now Capitol Avenue). The structure was built in 1888 at a cost of $4,000, and the lot cost $3,000. Inmate labor was used in constructing the building, which features nine-foot-high walnut pocket doors. Darwin W. Marmaduke was the first warden to occupy this residence. He was a brother of former Confederate major general John Sappington Marmaduke, who was governor of Missouri from 1885 to 1887. It was later used as the residence for the Missouri director of corrections. The warden's residence was later located at 722 East Capitol Avenue.

Thanks to an extensive private renovation project undertaken by Robert L. Hawkins, III, with local contractor Jude Markway, the mansion pictured here is still standing after nearly being demolished in the 1990s to make room for a parking lot. Sam'l H. Smith & Co., postcard 12803.

Housing Unit 4/A-Hall, pictured from the south. Warden Horace A. Swift designed A Hall. Inmate labor was used to construct the massive structure, built with blocks of stone quarried on the MSP property. The four-story structure had 152 cells and eight dungeon cells located below ground. At one time 744 inmates were crammed into A Hall. The plantings in the foreground were an attempt at creating a garden atmosphere behind the walls. Such themes became popular and were copied from prisons back East. Sam'l H. Smith & Co., postcard 12794, circa 1908.

At right, the main wall extends to one of 16 watchtowers. Towers were miserable places to be stationed; they were hot in the summer and freezing in the winter. The round towers, or castle turrets, were replaced following the 1954 riot with the round bases remaining.

Prison shops are at the left and, for the most part, they were sweat shops. Conditions were often unbearable, and the convicts worked for pennies each day. At one time there were five large shoe factories operating at the same time at MSP. A stamp and postmark cover the name of the postcard publisher, but it is thought that it was published by C. U. Williams, Bloomington, Illinois, postcard 13584.

Inmates leaving the dining hall. This card predates the early 1900s color-tinted postcards that show the courtyard with landscaping and flower beds. Published by C. U. Williams of Bloomington, Illinois, postcard 13565.

An early 1900s postcard of the Administration Building looking from the southwest. The building was later called H Hall and Housing Unit 1. The section where the windows appear in the foreground was the female unit. Social activists Kate Richards O'Hare and Emma Goldman did time in this unit around 1917–1920. No publishing information appears on this card.

The main courtyard, looking west, circa 1908. Note the two greenhouses at left. At center left, the Administration Building (women's unit). The deputy warden's office is at center and the hospital and Housing Unit 4/A Hall are at right. Published by Sam'l H. Smith & Co., postcard 12791.

The Isolation Building apparently was constructed about the time of World War I. Standing near old E Hall and the prison hospital, it was gone by 1935. This photo was printed for R. Dallmeyer Dry Goods Co., Jefferson City.

An early 1900s view of Housing Unit 4/A Hall, looking east, with the front door in view. This postcard was printed for the R. Dallmeyer Dry Goods Co., Jefferson City.

The main entrance wagon gate at MSP with the Administration Building on the right. The gate did exist; although, it appears to have been drawn on this postcard. The prison hospital is the red brick structure just to the right of the water tower. This postcard probably dates from the 1920s. Published by Curt Teich and Co., Chicago, postcard 12802

This view of the Administration Building is dated December 16, 1912. However, the photograph may have been taken earlier; notice the construction material near the front entrance by the team and wagon. At far left is the old prison hospital.

The Missouri Department of Natural Resources postcard to announce an exhibit of artifacts and images from MSP that took place at the Elizabeth Rozier Gallery in Jefferson City in 2007. The card shows an early 1900s image of the Administration Building.

The imposing Gothic Revival Administration Building, built in 1904–1905. Printed by the C. T. Company, Chicago, 1923.

Another postcard of the Administration Building, with the hospital and a watch tower beyond, circa 1913. Published by R. Dallmeyer Dry Goods Co., Jefferson City.

Lafayette Street ran in front of the original Administration Building until the gate entrance was constructed across the street. When the new Administration Building was constructed in the late 1930s, the front of the 1905 building was covered almost entirely. It was not exposed until the addition was removed in 2007 to make room for a new federal courthouse. Published by E. C. Kropp, Milwaukee, circa 1920.

A C. U. Williams Photoette postcard 13595 shows another angle of the Administration Building in the early 1900s. Note the horses and the buggy at left.

Visitors seem to be arriving at the old main entrance to the prison in this postcard. Note the buggy at left and the horse at extreme right. C. T. Company, Chicago, postcard, published by Sam'l H. Smith and Company, Jefferson City.

After fire destroyed the state capitol in February 1911, Missouri voted on a proposal to relocate the capital city. Feelings ran high as to whether another capitol would be built in the City of Jefferson, or if another city should receive the honor. Allegedly, Smith was a prison officer who voted "no" on the Jefferson City location and was hanged in effigy from a light pole.

A Photoette card, made by C. U. Williams, circa 1909, shows the interior of old E Hall, built in the 1880s (card 13583).

Convicts in striped pants march to the main dining hall. Striped uniforms were eliminated around 1912, except for the men assigned to the punishment hall. Note the greenhouse. Sam'l H. Smith & Co., Jefferson City, 1908, postcard 12793.

S. H. Kress published this photo of the 700 East Main (now Capitol Ave.) warden's residence, circa 1913. Parties, dances, and musical events were frequently held in the mansion.

The dining hall (left) and the newly built McClung Hall (later called Housing Unit 3/B & C Hall) (right), circa 1920. The iron fence at far left enclosed Housing Unit 4/A Hall (not shown). Note the courtyard's pool and fountain. Published by C. T. American Art, Chicago, postcard R-84267.

THE OUTCASTS HOME
ROY WILSON #23067
MISSOURI STATE PRISON
JEFFERSON CITY, MISSOURI

This postcard showing the interior of a cell appears to be from the 1920s or 1930s. Nothing is known of Roy Wilson or the purpose of the photo. Wilson apparently lived well in his small accommodation. There is an upper and a lower bunk at left. The ceiling light has a glass shade. A fan is on the small dresser at the rear of the cell. At right are two chairs, a table with a lamp, pictures, and other items. A carpet is on the floor.

Apparently, this was a holiday greeting card produced by MSP chaplain Edward Schluttman. It reads: "Season's Greetings, Noel 1947, Rev. Edw. D. Schluttman, Chaplain, Catholic Chapel, Missouri State Penitentiary." There may be more rare items like this tucked away in attics and basements.

Aerial view of MSP taken prior to the 1954 riot. The open area in the lower left is the prison ball field. It is believed that the early prison cemetery lies beneath it. The view is from southeast to northwest. Published by Gurwell News Agency, Jefferson City; printed by E. C. Kropp, Milwaukee (EDF, postcard 1933N).

A more recent postcard of the old Administration Building. The bust of Governor Alexander Monroe Dockery is visible above the entrance. The first-story brickwork and barred gateway were added about 1938 or 1939, during major remodeling at MSP. This gate was a main point of movement through the MSP Control Center lobby to other areas such as the prison hospital, which was outside the gate. Photographer and publisher unknown.

The main entrance gate and Administration Building. At left in the background is the five-floor hospital. All brick buildings were erected during the PWA and WPA era of the 1930s. Well-known Jefferson City photographer Zeal Wright, owner of Wright Studio and Camera Shop, took the photo. The postcard was made by Dexter Press, West Nyack, New York.

A rare copper officer's badge used in the 1900–1930 eras. Chris Hollaway photo.

A cane crudely carved and covered with dust is retrieved from the corner of a dark bedroom closet. No one notices the initials "MSP" carved into its walnut handle. A bureau drawer yields a wooden cigar box containing a brass whistle, an old badge of nickel silver and several brass tokens. Without hesitation the box and its contents are thrown into a dumpster. No one ever told the grandkids cleaning out the house that grandpa worked behind the walls of MSP for 30 years following World War I. No one really cared. And, so it goes, pieces of history are gone forever. The artifacts on the next several pages are not necessarily rare. They vary in monetary value. Each item had a history and a connection to the MSP story. If we don't save such items, what story will be told?

Staff-Related Items

In the early years, MSP officers wore no badges or patches. The badges on this page are from the twentieth century. Top row, left: rare copper badge worn sometime between 1900 and 1940. To the right of it is a rare assistant yard master's badge made of nickel and brass from about the same period. Third row: the small silver badge at right is an example of one purchased by an individual officer. Bottom row, left, is an executive assistant badge, an example of a specialized badge. This was worn inside a wallet or badge holder and could also be carried on a belt-clip badge holder. Third from the left is a small MSP E-Squad badge carried by members of the tactical unit. The small gold badge, second from right, is an example of one worn on the hat of a lieutenant or officer of higher rank. The small silver badge in the bottom row, right, was worn on the hat of an officer below the rank of lieutenant. *Chris Hollaway photo.*

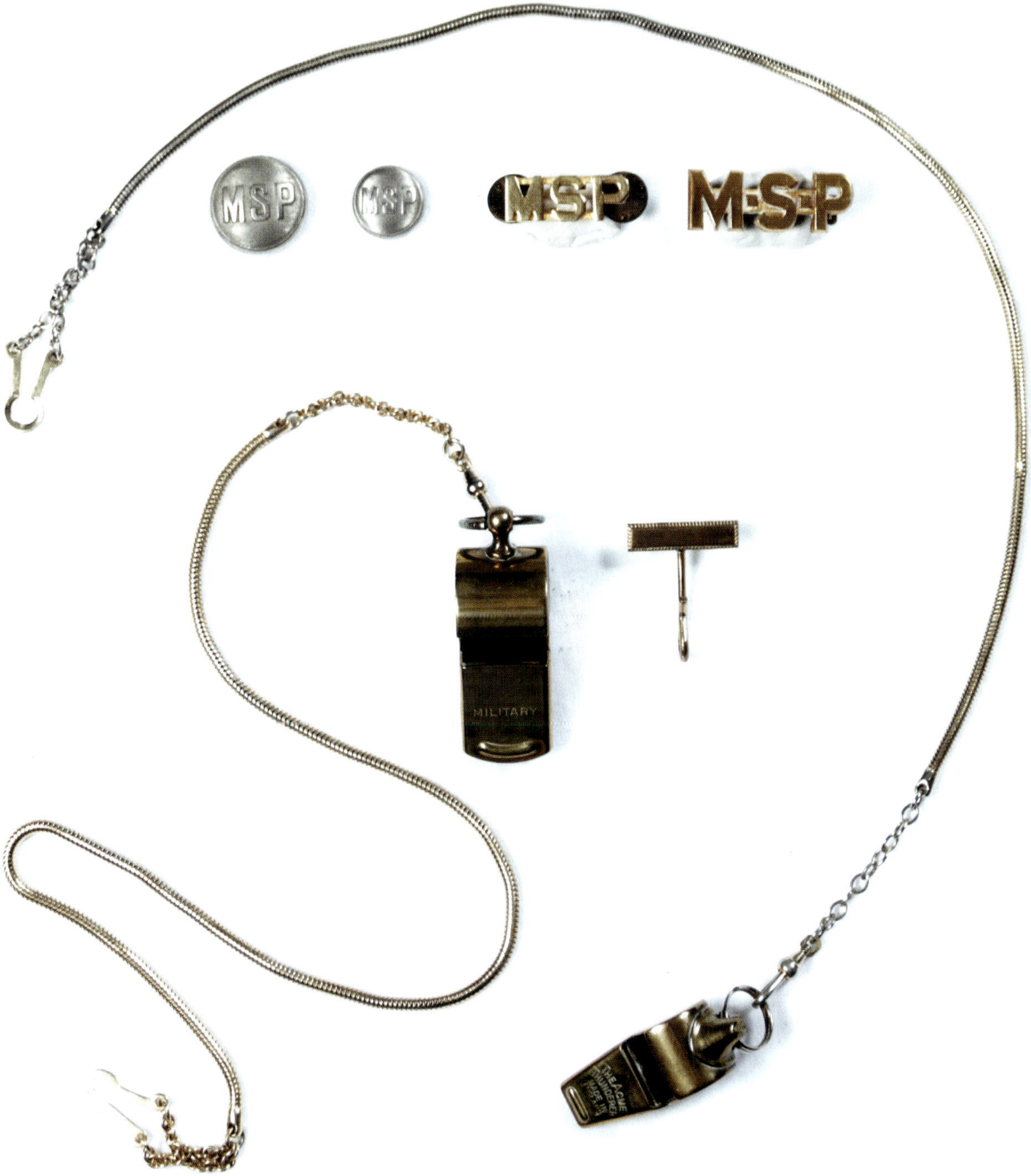

Buttons, pins, and whistles worn by officers. The coat buttons are rare and have not been worn for many years. The brass pins were worn by officers from the 1920s through the 1950s. Many old staff photos, like the one of officer (major) B.J. Poiry above, show the pins being worn on the lapel of a uniform coat or cap. The back of the MSP brass pins are stamped "S.G. Adams Co., St. Louis."

Whistles were used to signify that the perimeter towers were clear or that a staff member was in distress and in need of assistance. *Chris Hollaway and Lloyd Grotjan photos.*

Leather badge cases made for the staff by MSP inmates. The one with the initials MSS was made for the author in 1970 by an inmate named General David Parrish.

Bull's-eye lanterns were carried by MSP officers and staff from the time the prison opened in 1836. The massive buildings were like dark tombs until gas light, and later electricity, became available. This nineteenth- century lantern was originally owned by James Dunnica, who built the first MSP building between 1834 and 1836. He also built the first permanent capitol in Jefferson City. Dunnica was the great-great-great-grandfather of the author's wife.

An early battery-powered flashlight carried by an MSP officer. The brand name on the flashlight is Beacon. Officers supplied their own lights and other equipment, and many still purchase their own flashlights.

Chris Hollaway photos.

Missouri Department of Corrections staff have worn a variety of badges and patches over the years. The earliest patch style is the one at top left, which was worn during the 1954 prison riot. The Missouri prison system was first organized as the Missouri Department of Corrections in 1946. It lost its status as a department in 1974 and was renamed the Division of Corrections. In 1981, Corrections regained department status.

The two small green patches in the bottom row, left, were Emergency Squad patches. This unique unit was founded at MSP in the 1960s as a tactical response unit and was known as the E-Squad. Other Missouri Department of Corrections facilities later formed their own Emergency Squads.

From the 1960s through the 1980s, the members of the MSP E-Squad elected their members, subject to the approval of the warden and deputy warden, who served as administrative commanders. It was considered an honor to belong to this squad. The unit was formed by Deputy Warden Donald Wyrick, later the warden of MSP, and Captain Danton Steele, later Major Steele, to prepare the MSP staff for a variety of emergency situations. Warden Wyrick did not want a repeat of an unprepared staff that experienced the riot of September 22, 1954. Original MSP E-Squad patches are now rare.

Bottom row, extreme right: a rare MSP Fire and Rescue Squad patch. Formed on the same principle as the E-Squad, the Fire and Rescue Squad could respond to a variety of emergencies. Fires were not uncommon in early years. *Chris Hollaway photo.*

Modern uniform patches worn by Missouri Department of Corrections staff. The K-9 patch at bottom is no longer used.

Uniform belt with shoulder strap used by staff. The exact time period for this accessory is unknown but is believed to be from the 1920s and 1930s. *Courtesy Mr. and Mrs. Allen L. Sartain.*

Chris Hollaway photos.

Officer's hat worn from the 1960s through the mid-1980s. The gold band and gold badge denote a rank of lieutenant or above. In the early years, MSP officers had no specific headwear, badges, or insignia to make them stand out. There were no uniforms for staff; street clothes were worn, and no doubt they were of poor quality, because staff were often not paid for weeks or months at a time.

As conditions improved slightly, staff began to wear bowler or derby style hats, trousers, and coats. By the 1930s, blue serge suits were required for officers, and old photos show them wearing a uniform cap with an oval badge on the front. Their dark blue caps were similar to the style seen here.

A felt uniform hat worn during the winter months. Officers would have used a gold cord, and the badge would have been attached through the hole at the front of the hat. The hole in the hat brim was for a hat strap to help secure it to one's head. Corrections officers through the rank of sergeant wore a silver badge.

A straw hat was worn with the green uniform that was standard issue in the 1960s and 1970s. In the 1980s, brown baseball-style caps were worn during the summer months. An "Ike" style green jacket was worn in warm months, and a heavy green wool coat was issued for winter.

Lieutenants and higher-ranking officers wore gold braid or piping around the sleeves of their uniform jackets. One stripe was for a lieutenant, two stripes for a captain, and so on. Rank insignia were also worn on the collar of the uniform shirt, and sergeant stripes were worn on the shoulder of the shirt. Lieutenants and above wore the gold hat badge. The gold cord and cap badge on this hat denote a ranking officer. Initially, the uniform shirts worn by officers were light tan or brown. Later, ranking officers were issued white shirts.

Chris Hollaway photos.

An original standard-issue tan uniform shirt with a Department of Corrections patch, a clip-on necktie, and a whistle with original lanyard. The shoulder patch is a newer issue; note the name "Missouri Department of Corrections and Human Resources." This name was not used until after the 1970s and was later eliminated.

Before portable radios were introduced into the prison, the whistle was standard issue and was the only means of communication between officers. The Acme Thunderer whistle made in England was used at MSP as late as the 1970s. If a fight or stabbing took place or an escape attempt was unfolding, officers blew whistles to sound the alert and to summon assistance. Before an intercom system was installed, tower officers were required to go out on the tower catwalk and blow their whistles every fifteen minutes. This was done in numerical sequence, starting with Tower 1 and progressing around the wall.

The whistle later became more of a symbol. Although it could still be used, it was worn as a nostalgic piece of old MSP's colorful past. The cord lanyard gave way to more ornate styles made of gold cord, small chains, and so on. A standard joke at MSP was, "Hey, Joe, I heard you were in a fight on the upper yard with several cons. Did you blow the pee [not pea] out of your whistle?" The clip-on tie was superior to older hand-tied styles, which were dangerous. On more than one occasion an angry inmate grabbed an officer by the tie and attempted to choke him. Clip-ons simply came off in the aggressor's hand. *Chris Hollaway photo.*

A few of the many booklets and pamphlets issued by MSP and the Missouri Department of Corrections. Most contain rules and regulations for staff and inmates. The two custodial and training manuals at upper left belonged to Captain Leroy Casey. These are courtesy of Allen Sartain, former MSP training officer and son-in-law of Captain Casey. Jim Dallas contributed a number of manuals and written material about MSP probation and parole to the Missouri State Archives. *Chris Hollaway photo.*

An Iver-Johnson .22 cal. pistol, carried by Captain Buck Williams in the early part of the twentieth century. The item could be easily concealed on the person. Staff was always outnumbered by the inmate population and carried such weapons in case they would be needed. In reality, having them inside the prison created a greater danger. *Chris Hollaway photo.*

At first glance, these look like 19 canes. Instead, they are linesticks carried by high-ranking officers and supervisors inside MSP. Early photos, some from the 1930s, show staff with these sticks, which were a tool of authority. No two were exactly alike, as each was custom made for the owner.

Most were made at the Sullivan Saddle Tree Factory; however, later, a few were made in one of the prison's shoe factories. All include a flexible metal rod or shaft that ran the entire length of the stick; the rod was then covered with small pieces of leather, each glued to the other. Various types of inlaid material, usually shell, were added to personalize the stick. Several have the owner's initials inlaid. Sometimes brass was used on the handle end or at the tip of the stick.

The linesticks were not weight-bearing because of the flexibility of the metal rod. They were used to direct convict lines, marching in silent lockstep to different locations within the prison. A supervisor would simply hold up his linestick and point to the lead man, and the line would move in automated motion. If the staff person felt threatened, or if someone didn't move fast enough or failed to obey a directive, the linestick with its flexible rod could be used on the inmate's body to bring about compliance.

For many years some local antique dealers in Jefferson City thought the items were just canes. In more than one instance the author made the mistake of informing them of the item's history, and consequently the price skyrocketed. *Chris Hollaway and Julie Woodman photos.*

Canes made by inmates. The top and bottom canes were used by an old inmate who was nicknamed "Bang-Bang Brookshire." He would point his cane at an individual and yell, "Bang, bang, you're dead!" The canes were finally taken from him after he struck several individuals. He was in prison for murdering one of his hired hands who had worked on his Central Missouri farm. At one time, Brookshire had been a member of the Missouri General Assembly.

The second cane from the top was made by inmate Shelby Debler, a master craftsman who carved this beautiful piece from mahogany. The handle is from a stainless steel medical instrument that belonged to the late Dr. Lawrence E. Giffen, who was a much-loved physician, a Cole County medical examiner, and an avid historian.

The cane at second from the bottom belonged to an inmate known as "German Bob" who made it at MSP during the 1970s. Inmates often made canes in the factories for their own use, stating that they needed help in walking. Usually the canes were made as an item of defense and were considered contraband. Inmates who genuinely needed a cane were provided one by the medical department.

One of the most beautiful canes was owned by Warden Harold R. Swenson. It was very ornate, with likenesses of men carved on it, and was made for him by an inmate whose name has been lost. It is not known what became of his beautiful piece of prison art. *Chris Hollaway photo.*

An early MSP staff identification card. Charles J. Tritsch was a native of Jefferson City. Both his father and grandfather worked as foremen inside the walls. Upon returning from the U.S. Army following World War II, he worked as an officer at the prison. The I.D. shown was glued to a blue cardboard cover. Very few of these still exist. *Courtesy Ron and Cheryl Tritsch, children of Charles.*

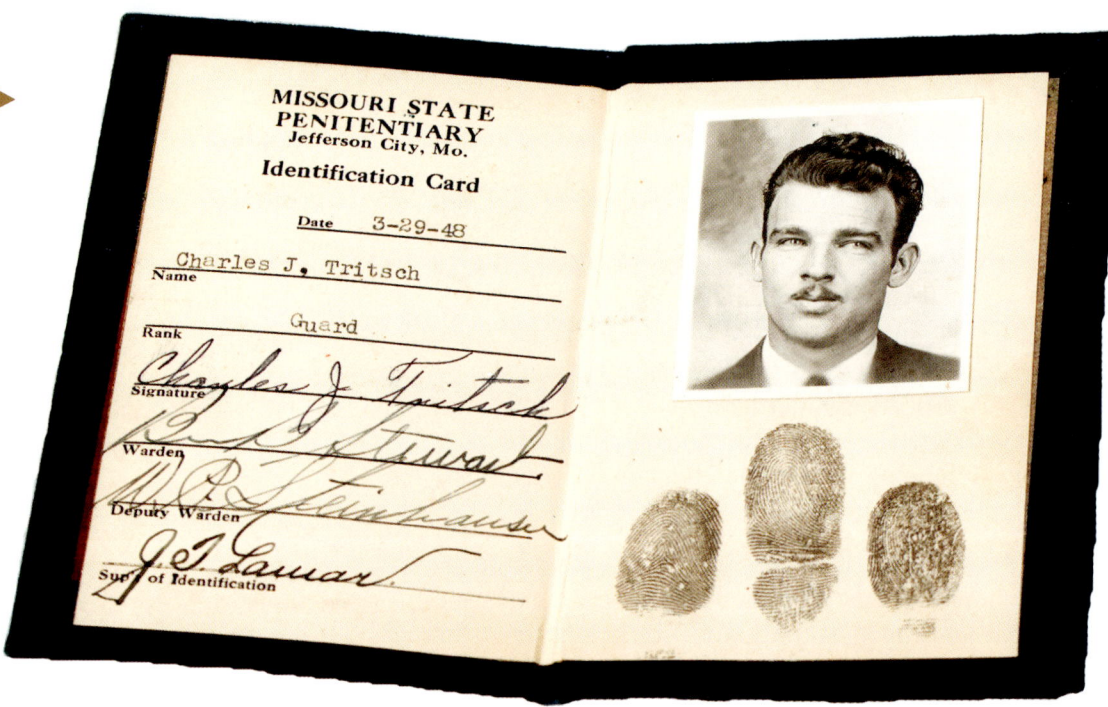

Whether you call them batons, billy clubs, or nightsticks, many dozens like these and others were made for staff over the years. These two were turned in the prison furniture factory. Billy clubs were carried as defensive and enforcement equipment. They were phased out by the late 1960s, but commercially manufactured ones were still available. *Chris Hollaway photo.*

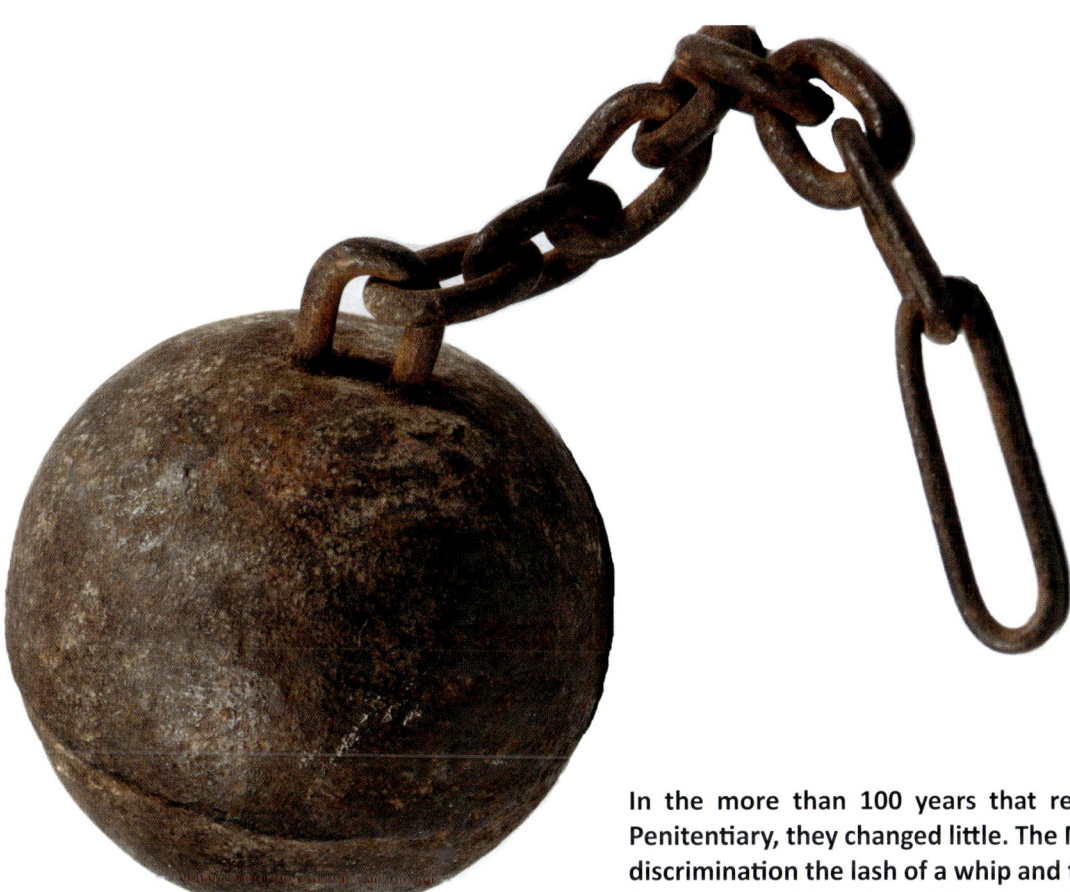

A nineteenth-century ball and chain. A portion of the chain is missing, including the section which clamped around the ankle. The ball and chain was used as a restraining device both within the prison and on men who worked on outside details. Chris Hollaway photo.

In the more than 100 years that restraint and locking devices were used at the Missouri State Penitentiary, they changed little. The MSP embraced the harsh Auburn System that employed without discrimination the lash of a whip and the infamous cat-of-nine-tails. As one convict would later relate, "men were whipped until blood filled their shoes." Some did not survive. Manacles and shackles of various designs were placed on unfortunate men and secured to the rings in the dungeon cells of the MSP. The use of the ball and chain and the Oregon Boot was not uncommon. From the beginning, staff carried a variety of weapons ranging from clubs, truncheons, billys, nightsticks, batons, brass knuckles and line sticks to knives and firearms. Many were unauthorized, but heads turned and looked the other way. Locking devices initially were crude and consisted of padlocks and chains. Large keys operated door locks. As time progressed, locks became more complex. Weapons carried by staff, with the exception of firearms, remained almost unchanged. The following pages exhibit a few unique artifacts that were used to ensure compliance at the old MSP. There are, no doubt, many more tucked away in closets, attics, and drawers, waiting to have their chapter of MSP history related.

Restraint & Locking Devices

Several types of early restraints. The pair of handcuffs at the top-middle has a key lock missing. They are stamped 73626 and 73636. The restraints at lower right have no visible markings. The restraints at extreme right are marked "Tower Double Lock." *Chris Hollaway photo.*

Curving around top and left, a long chain used for securing hand or ankle-leg restraints around the waist. The three restraints in the center are handcuffs, and the ones curving at lower right and bottom are ankle shackles. Smaller restraints were used at MSP to secure female prisoners who were imprisoned there from 1842 until 1926.

The handcuffs at top center have no visible manufacturer's name on them but do have a patent date of November 28, 1882. The handcuffs at center left were used in the 1960s and 1970s and are from the Peerless Handcuff Company Springfield, Massachusetts. They are marked MSP 82-8. The odd-shaped hand restraints at right center are marked "Mfg. by Mattatuck Mfg. Co. Waterbury, Conn." The restraints curving at right and bottom are marked "H & R Arms Co., Worcester, MA." *Chris Hollaway photo.*

This brass-and-leather baton is an excellent example of the craftsmanship of the inmates. Well-crafted clubs like this were often given to high-ranking or long-term officers. The leather rings were glued in place. This was probably made between 1890 and 1930.
Chris Hollaway photo.

Although not as ornate as the one above, this billy club is another example of craftsmanship demonstrated by inmates. It, too, likely dates from 1890 to 1930.
Chris Hollaway photo.

An almost endless variation of billy clubs, batons, night sticks, saps, and slappers were used throughout MSP's history. Left to right: two blackjacks made with lead-weighted tips wrapped with leather. Next, a club made of lead wrapped in heavy cloth tape. The fourth club from the left is weighted, with a braided handle and wrist cord. Fifth and sixth from left, clubs of sewn leather filled with powdered lead. The next two clubs (center) are more ornate, consisting of brass and leather. These were handcrafted by inmates at the MSP and were carried until after the 1954 prison riot. The ninth item is a specialized handcrafted presentation billy club made of walnut. It was crafted by inmate Roy Engberg. The black leather slapper or sap was used after the riot and was issued to specific staff during the 1960s and 1970s. The black leather gloves at extreme right were not standard issue. They were manufactured and sold by law enforcement equipment companies. The gloves are weighted with powdered lead in the knuckles.

Knuckles like these were carried by some staff members. Some were of brass, and they came in a variety of sizes.

Chris Hollaway photo.

The small pair of field glasses was carried by tower officers to view activity in the prison yard and along the wall. If officers wanted to use field glasses, they supplied their own. In later years the glasses were state-issued equipment.

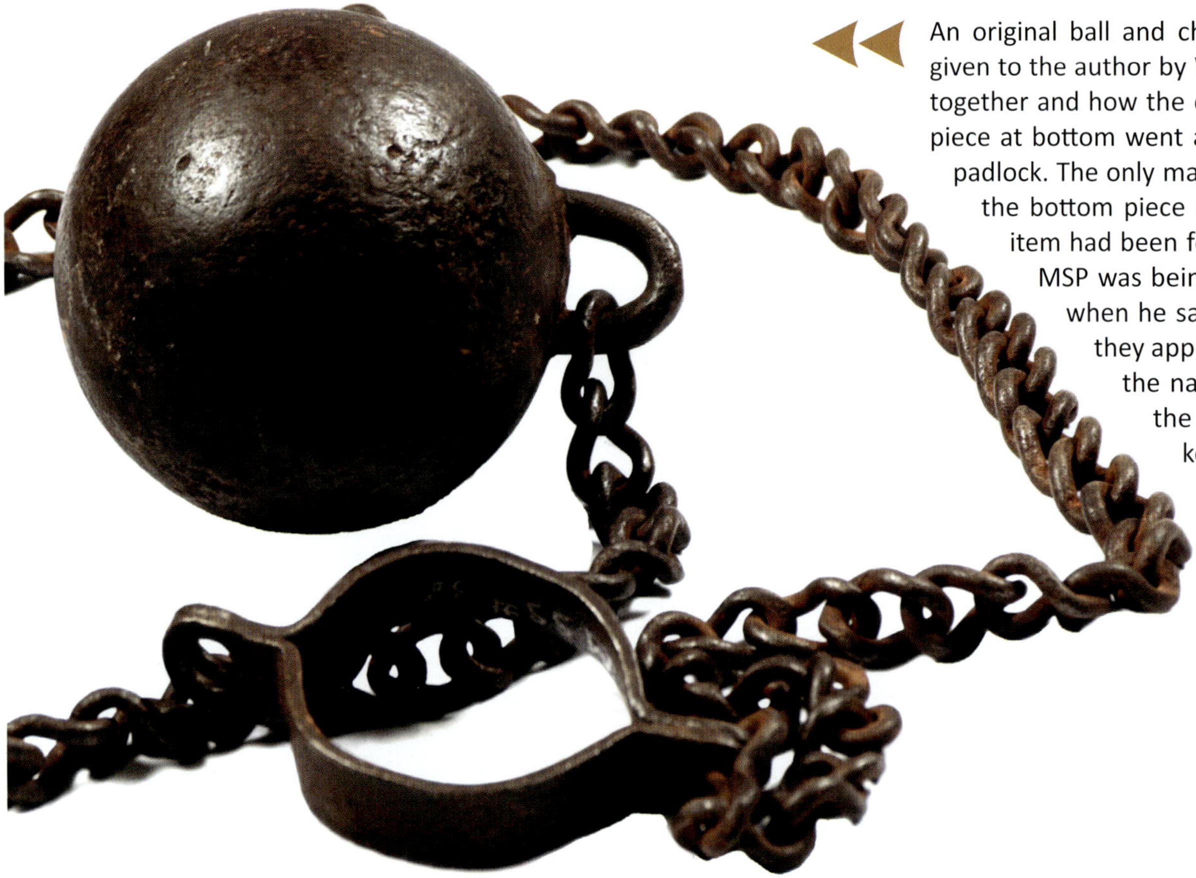

An original ball and chain used at the Missouri State Penitentiary. It was given to the author by Warden Harold R. Swenson. Note how the item is put together and how the chain links have been made and joined together. The piece at bottom went around the inmate's leg and was secured by a heavy padlock. The only markings on the item are those placed by the author on the bottom piece as a reference number. Warden Swenson stated the item had been found buried under dirt and debris when old E-Hall at MSP was being torn down. It was being taken to the prison dump when he saved it. Collectors should beware of such items when they appear for sale on the internet. Many junk items will have the name of a notorious prison stamped on them to make the item appear genuine. The same applies to badges, keys, and locks. *Chris Hollaway photo.*

Seen here are two well-used Folger Adam keys. They are joined with a screw and nut. In many instances the prison's locksmith made or redesigned keys at the MSP. *Chris Hollaway photo.*

An "Oregon Boot" that is broken down into its various components. The author was given this rare item by former MSP Warden Harold R. Swenson. Swenson stated that he had obtained the item from an MSP officer who used it as a doorstop. The two large sections at the top and the piece at bottom right fit together around an inmate's leg. The two wooden-handled ratchet devices shown at lower left fit into the holes seen in the upper left section. When this item was tightened, the leg piece was securely locked around the inmate's leg. The brace piece at lower right fit inside the upper section and went around the leg. The flattened bottom of the device at lower right was screwed to the inmate's shoe heel. When he walked he had to swing his leg because the boot was so heavy. *Chris Hollaway photo.*

The Oregon Boot with pieces fit together, with the ratchet pieces in position for securing the device. The section at right looks much like a leg brace. It went around the leg of the prisoner and on the inside of the piece at the left. Note the screw holes that would attach the restraint to the inmate's shoe. *Chris Hollaway photo.*

Through the long history of the Missouri State Penitentiary, numerous locking devices and keys were used. Several hundred keys were used by staff each day to operate the institution. The prison had a full-time locksmith and, on several occasions, more than one. The lock shop held hundreds of blank and backup keys as well as lock parts, spare locking devices, and tools used by the locksmith.

Housing unit officers often carried several pounds of keys. Before the prison closed in 2004, it was not uncommon for the locksmith to make lock parts, because the companies that had made the original locks no longer existed. Seen here are Folger, Adam, Stewart, and Cleveland 4-Way keys commonly used in the prison. The small key at bottom center is an antique handcuff key. *Chris Hollaway photo.*

More keys and locking devices used at the Missouri State Penitentiary. The keys at bottom right are Stewart keys. None of the keys used at MSP were stamped with the prison name when they were received from the manufacturer. In later years, MSP locksmiths marked the keys by placing a metal tab on the key ring for identification. Collectors should be very careful when purchasing keys marked with prison names. *Courtesy Warden Dave Dormire. Chris Hollaway photo.*

◀◀ Styles of locks and locking devices varied in the prison. By the time MSP closed, many were so old that prison locksmiths were having to craft parts to repair them, as manufactured parts were no longer available.

At center is a door-locking device.

The large padlock at upper left is marked "Segal."

The lock at lower right was alleged to have been broken when MSP inmates Edward Raymond, George Ryan, Harry Vaughan, and Hiram Blake shot and used nitroglycerin to blow their way out during an escape in 1905. It was handed down in the family of John G. Tritsch, a foreman at the J. S. Sullivan Saddle Tree Factory. *Chris Hollaway photo.*

A wristband crafted from a piece of a leather boot. Upholstery nails were inserted through the leather with the sharp points sticking out. The inmate from whom this was confiscated had several of these that he had made. Tied around each wrist of a fighter, such weapons could inflict painful injuries to an unsuspecting opponent. Chris Hollaway photo.

Dangerous contraband is always a concern in any prison. Any item or substance that may cause or result in physical injury or death to a person is dangerous contraband. Items classified as such may vary in a prison environment. The threat posed by a knife or firearm is obvious. Deodorant containing alcohol that can be used as napalm is not so obvious. Paper clips, dental floss, hairpins, toilet paper, and a ball-point pen may all be altered to become dangerous contraband. Circumstances alter cases. Shown in this section are photographs of dangerous contraband items recovered at the MSP. They demonstrate the ingenuity, creativity, and skill of many who served time behind the walls. Even dangerous contraband has a story that contributes to the social history of American prisons.

Contraband: Dangerous

1. Lethal knives can be fashioned from a great variety of materials. This knife was made from a file, and the handle was from a weight machine. The author recovered this weapon during a search of Housing Unit 4/A Hall. As officers approached the area, the weapon was thrown from an upper tier. It nearly hit the author, who was positioned below watching the movement of inmates on the upper tier. The knife is 11½" long.

2. This knife was given to the author by the family of Major Danton G. Steele, chief of custody at MSP during the 1960s and early 1970s. The weapon is made from a piece of flat steel. File marks can be seen on the blade. It is well crafted and has a handle of masking tape. A masking tape sheath rests under the knife, which is 11½" long.

3. A knife made from the handle of a portable radio, with a masking-tape handle, 11" long. Recovered by the author.

4. A large knife made from a piece of flat steel from the MSP machine shop. Holes were drilled through the steel, and handles were fashioned from walnut taken from the MSP furniture factory and screwed together. This knife is 14½" long and was recovered by the author.

5. A grinder was used in making this knife, but the temper was not taken out of the steel, for it is not discolored (which often occurs when a grinder is used). The handle is made from wood wrapped with adhesive tape. Length is 11".

6. A small, very sharp knife made from flat steel. The walnut handles were attached with screws. Length is 9½".

7. The first knife recovered by the author, in 1968. It was found in the baseball dugout at MSP's Ozark Stadium. It was made from a steel shop ruler with a handle of black electrical tape. The numbers are visible on the ruler. Length is 12".

Chris Hollaway photos.

From left: a spike-type weapon made from a 13" welding rod; a sharpened paint roller handle; a unique spike-type weapon made from electric fan guards with a handle made of melted plastic, cardboard, and shoelaces; and a boning knife taken from the cold storage area and resharpened.

The fifth item from the left is the handle from a broken food-service ladle that was sharpened to a point. Next, a broken crescent wrench sharpened to a point. The discoloration of the metal indicates that a grinder was used.

The knife seventh from left was recovered by the author and has an ice pick point inserted into a walnut handle with a carved face. Next is a saw-blade style weapon inserted into a crude cardboard handle wrapped with duct tape.

Next is a weapon made from sharpened plastic; the handle is wrapped with an elastic bandage and black electrical tape.

The green arrowhead-shaped push-pull weapon was made commercially of high-impact-resistant material. This item was brought into the institution from outside. Weapons made from such materials are difficult to detect.

Below, the star-shaped device was made from melted plastic with nails. Although not lethal, it could inflict a painful wound.

Next, an unusual arrow harpoon was bolted to a longer shaft attached to a rope. The harpoon was to be thrown or fired at a tower officer while he stood on an outside catwalk, knocking him off, so that the escapees could grab his sidearm and escape over the high stone wall. This and other items were to have been used in an elaborate escape plot, circa 1980.

The fourth weapon from the right had the potential to inflict lethal wounds. It is made from a cigarette lighter with a piece of stiff wire forced into it. Length is 6".

The next weapon was recovered by the author in 1981 from beneath the pillow of an inmate sent to Missouri from New Mexico. It was made from a large stainless steel serving spoon and sharpened to a point at the end of the handle. The bowl of the spoon was bent so that the weapon could be easily handled. Length is 13¾".

A knife made from a heavy piece of steel broken from a window-opening device. A crank was turned to open the windows, and the cogs on the long metal pieces worked like gears to open multiple windows. This weapon was sharpened and had gray duct tape wrapped around the handle. It came from Housing Unit 3/B & C Hall and is 10¼" long.

At far right, a weapon made from a paste ink measuring ruler used on a factory machine. The handle is made from masking tape, and a shoestring is at the end to secure the weapon to the hand. Length is 11¼". *Chris Hollaway photos.*

Six weapons fashioned from plastic. Some are more crude than others; all are deadly.

The third weapon from the top, 9" in length, was discovered on an inmate who was going out of the prison to court.

The weapon at far lower left was made from a plastic butter knife. Plastic knives had replaced the metal ones, but they, too, became a problem and were discontinued. *Chris Hollaway photo.*

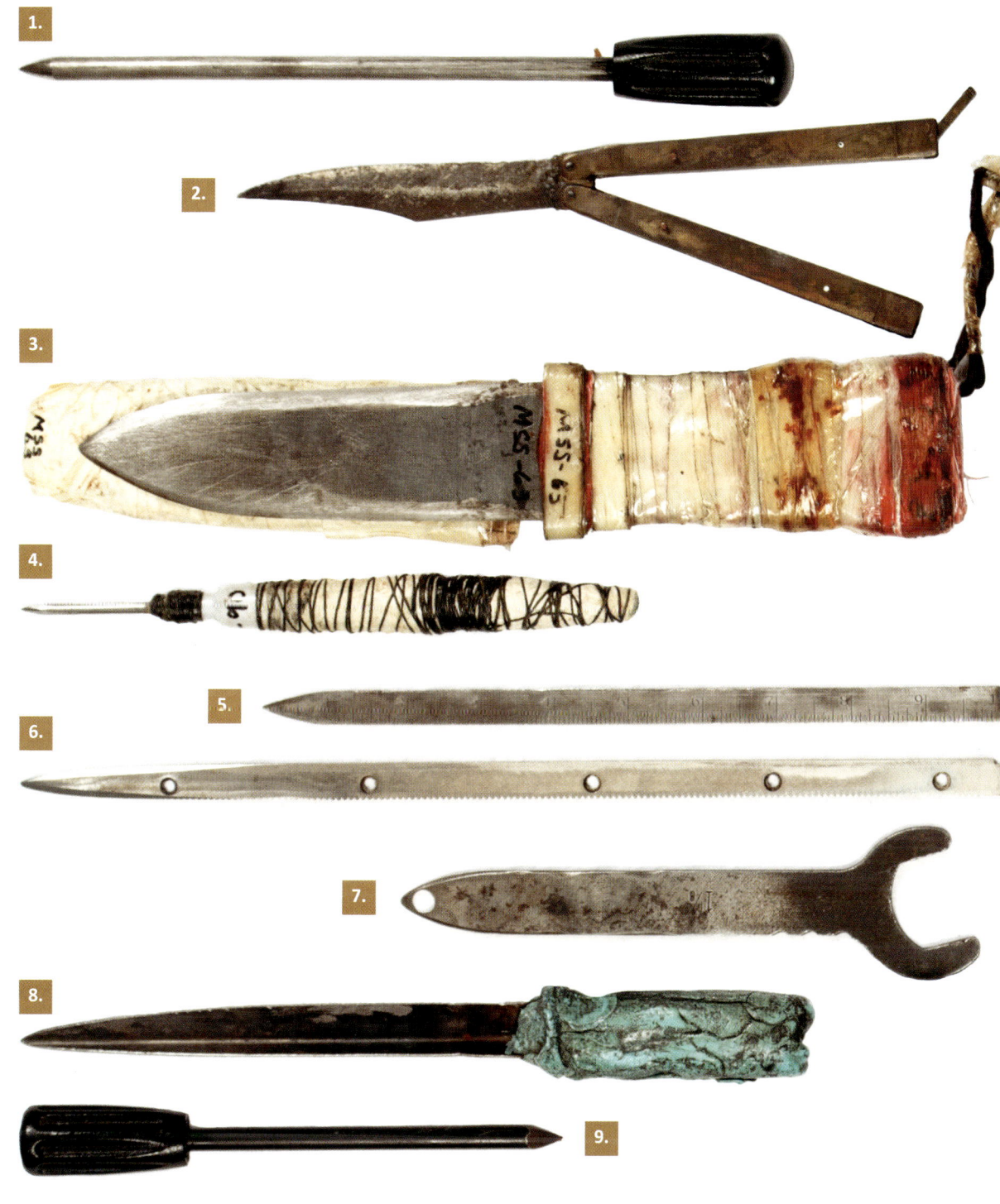

1. & 9. A weapon made from the adjustment lever of an office chair. Length is 10". The item at the bottom of this page was made from the same thing.

2. An antique butterfly-style knife with brass handles. The blade folds into the two handles. Note the locking device on the end of the upper handle. This weapon opens with a flip of the wrist and is 9½" long. It was hidden in a wall of Housing Unit 4/A Hall.

3. A wide knife made from heavy-gauge steel from the metal plant. Both edges of the blade have been filed sharp. The handle is made of cardboard and strapping tape. The shoestring attached to the handle could be wrapped around the wrist or hand so the weapon would not be dropped during a fight. Sometimes tape would be used to secure a weapon to the hand of a fighter. The blade length is 12"; blade width is 1¾". Note the sheath, made of cardboard and tape.

4. This small weapon was made from a Magic Marker and a nail. Tape and heavy thread were used as reinforcement. Although crude, the weapon was dangerous. It was recovered in Housing Unit 3/D. Length is 8¼".

5. & 6. Two weapons made from typewriter parts. The one on the top is 10" long and was made from a typewriter gauge. The one below is 13¾" long. Inmates filed civil actions against the prison administrative staff to obtain typewriters for legal work. Thirty-one weapons made from typewriter pieces were recovered.

7. This crescent wrench was sharpened into a 7¾" weapon.

8. A dangerous weapon made from a piece of metal bracing material. A melted plastic cup was secured to the metal to form a handle. Length is 10".

Chris Hollaway photos.

◀◀

Standard butter or table knives were easily altered to make weapons. The table knife at center is unaltered. Such knives were used in the dining rooms at MSP through the 1970s. More stabbings took place using these knives, and more weapons were made from them than from any other material at MSP. Note the weapon with the red bandana and shoestring handle. All are 8½" long. *Chris Hollaway photo.*

1. A weapon made of two pieces of steel welded together. Note the cut-out sections where fingers could grip the knife. Length is 8¼".

2. This knife was made from very heavy plastic that was simply shaved down. Length is 9½".

3. The handle of this small knife was made from a melted deodorant container.

4. A simple 7" weapon fashioned from a bent margin bar of a typewriter. The handle is made from black electrical tape.

5. An unusual knife made from a steak bone. It was recovered in 1982 from the Supermax unit. It has a piece of sheet wrapped around it for a handle. Length is 5".

6. An oddly shaped weapon of heavy-gauge steel. The blade has been filed to a sharp edge, and black tape was used for the handle. Length is 5½".

7. A garrote weapon consisting of wire and two wooden handles. Length is 10". Weapons similar to this were used in several strangulation homicides at MSP. Dental floss can also be made into a very strong garrote.

8. A most effective weapon can be created with half of a pair of scissors. Tape was added to aid in holding the weapon securely. Length is 10". The author investigated several assaults and homicides at MSP where scissor weapons were used.

9. What appears to be a very small weapon extends to a greater length. The small button is pushed to release a spring-loaded blade. This device was recovered in the old administrative segregation and death row unit. Length, closed, is 5"; extended length is 7¾".

10. This 8" weapon was originally the handle from a portable radio.

Chris Hollaway photos.

1. This weapon was found in the cast of an inmate patient at the MSP hospital. The handle was wrapped with adhesive tape.

2. Components for making a .22 caliber zip gun. Although rendered inoperable when recovered, this item was deadly. The barrel could be unscrewed and the weapon disassembled. This tactic is frequently used in prisons to make it more difficult to locate contraband items.

3. A chisel has been worked into a point to create this weapon, 5½" long.

4. A knife made from a serving spoon handle. Strapping tape was used for the handle.

5. An odd weapon made from the rings of a binder notebook. Cloth was wrapped around the device for a handle.

6. This needle-type weapon was recovered by the author on the fifth-floor mental ward of the old MSP hospital. It is extremely sharp. The handle is made from old cloth adhesive tape. Blue tape wrapped around cardboard constitutes the sheath. The weapon had been wrapped in clear plastic so the offender could conceal it in his rectum. Length is 6".

7. A small weapon with a wooden handle made from popsicle sticks and a very small commercially made knife that was inserted into the handle. The handle was wrapped with wire to give it strength. Length is 6¼".

8. Although the inmate who made this weapon from a bent fork insisted it was a back scratcher, the item was seized as dangerous contraband nonetheless. The fork handle was inserted into a piece of wood and wrapped with black tape. Length is 9½".

9. Here, a piece of metal strip was secured by two wooden handles. Holes were drilled through the metal strip. The weapon was not suitable for stabbing, but it was an ideal slashing weapon. Length is 12½".

10. Not many contraband knives are constructed with a hilt guard to protect the user's hand. Black electrical tape was wrapped around the handle. Length is 9½".
Chris Hollaway photos.

1. A small cutting blade has been inserted into the end of a pencil and reinforced with tape. Length is 6½"; blade is 1". The pencil was from the Central Missouri Trust Company, Jefferson City.

2. A piece of fan guard, inserted into a cigarette lighter. The plastic of the lighter was melted so the metal could be inserted. Length is 5".

3. A spike weapon fashioned from an awl-type tool. The steel handle was welded to the shank. The weapon resembles a push-pull dagger. Length is 5".

4. A small double-bladed knife found inside a hollowed-out Bible at MSP in 1981. The blades fold into a round disk made of brass with a faux pearl handle. The blades are stamped "Ambassador." Length is 2".

5. A Bic ballpoint pen with a screwdriver blade inserted into it. The device would not generally be considered dangerous contraband; however, it had been altered and was in the possession of an inmate who was known for his escape attempts. Such devices are a major concern in prisons. It was determined that an inmate was using the screwdriver to remove security screws inside his cell.

6. Toothbrush weapons are commonly found in prisons. Often a razor blade or other sharp materials are inserted into melted plastic. A nail was used in this instance. Length is 5". Very short toothbrushes are now used in many prisons.

7. This small knife was created by joining an old knife blade to a reworked screwdriver handle. Length is 3¾".

8. A box-opening knife, designed to be worn on an index finger. The blade is very sharp. This type of item was never used in the MSP. How it made its way into the prison, no one knows. Blade length is 1".

9. A small commercial knife that was smuggled into MSP. The handle was absent, so a new one was made using glue and twine. Length is 6". *Chris Hollaway photos.*

◄◄ This blade was taken from a planing machine in the MSP furniture factory. The edge was razor sharp on both sides and the steel is very hard. The handles are welded on. Length is 13".

◄◄ This double-bladed axe was one of several similar axes recovered at MSP. The men who made and possessed them were members of the "Aryan Brotherhood," a militant white supremacist prison organization. The weapons resemble those carried by early Vikings. Workmanship was crude, but the blades were extremely sharp.

◄◄ An oak-handled weapon recovered by the author in the MSP furniture factory. The inmate who had the weapon operated a saw. At times he took the weapon apart keeping the blade at his workstation and the handle elsewhere. This helped to avoid detection, since he was authorized to have the blade at his work site. On the day the author found the weapon, the inmate had made the serious mistake of having the two pieces assembled as shown in the photo. Length is 16¼".

◄◄ Another heavy, skillfully made weapon. The blade is razor sharp and is welded to a solid steel handle. Tape was used on the handle so the weapon would not easily slip from the hand while being swung. Length is 17¼". Recovered in Housing Unit 2/F & G Hall.

◄◄ A well-crafted axe made from heavy steel, one of the more unique items recovered at MSP. The blade was created from the baseplate (shoe) of an iron. Time and skill were required to bevel the edge of the blade. The long heavy handle was securely bolted to the baseplate. Length is 21¾"; the blade is 7¾" long and 4¾" wide.

Chris Hollaway photos.

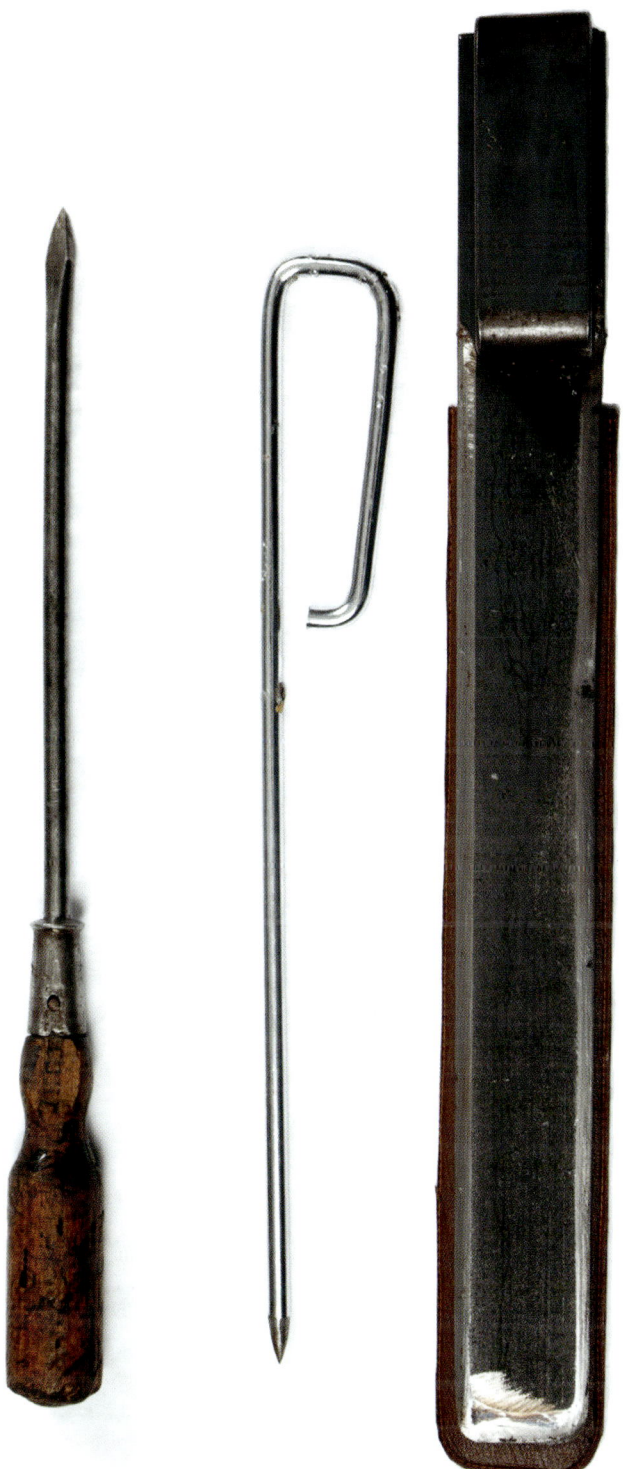

Left: a sharpened screwdriver; length is 16¼". This is a prime example of why all materials and tools must be accurately inventoried and accounted for. Failure to do so is a major breach of institutional security.

Center: a long stainless steel weapon was made from a piece of oven rack. Length is 15".

Right: large, heavy weapon made for slashing and hacking rather than stabbing. The blade is a piece of thick, heavy steel. The handle was skillfully welded to the blade. Both sides and the end of the blade have been honed to a razor-sharp edge. Length is 19". The sheath lies under the blade. Recovered by the author from under an ice chest. MSP staff found two other almost identical weapons.

The fabricated knuckles were recovered from a hole found in a cell in Housing Unit 2/F &G Hall.

Chris Hollaway photos.

One of the most dangerous offenders to ever walk through the doors of MSP made the fake .25 cal. pistol shown. Not long before the recovery of this item and another like it, this inmate, along with another, had taken staff members hostage in Housing Unit 1/H Hall in a desperate escape attempt. The incident was resolved after approximately six hours, and no one was injured. During the initial hostage situation the two inmates involved had real firearms and a small cutting torch, which an investigation traced to an MSP employee. The fake pistol shown was so realistic that it had "Charter Arms" and a serial number on it. The hollow book in which it was placed came from the MSP law library. As a result of this incident, and a later hostage incident, the inmate was assigned to Administrative Segregation where he remained for 16 years. *Julie Woodman photo.*

Components of a prison pipe shotgun manufactured from fittings found in the prison plumbing shop. The barrel at the bottom is 20" long. The firing pin is at middle; its length is 8¾". Assembled length is 27". The item is no longer operable and has been dismantled. Several of these were recovered at MSP during the 1970s and early 1980s. *Chris Hollaway photo.*

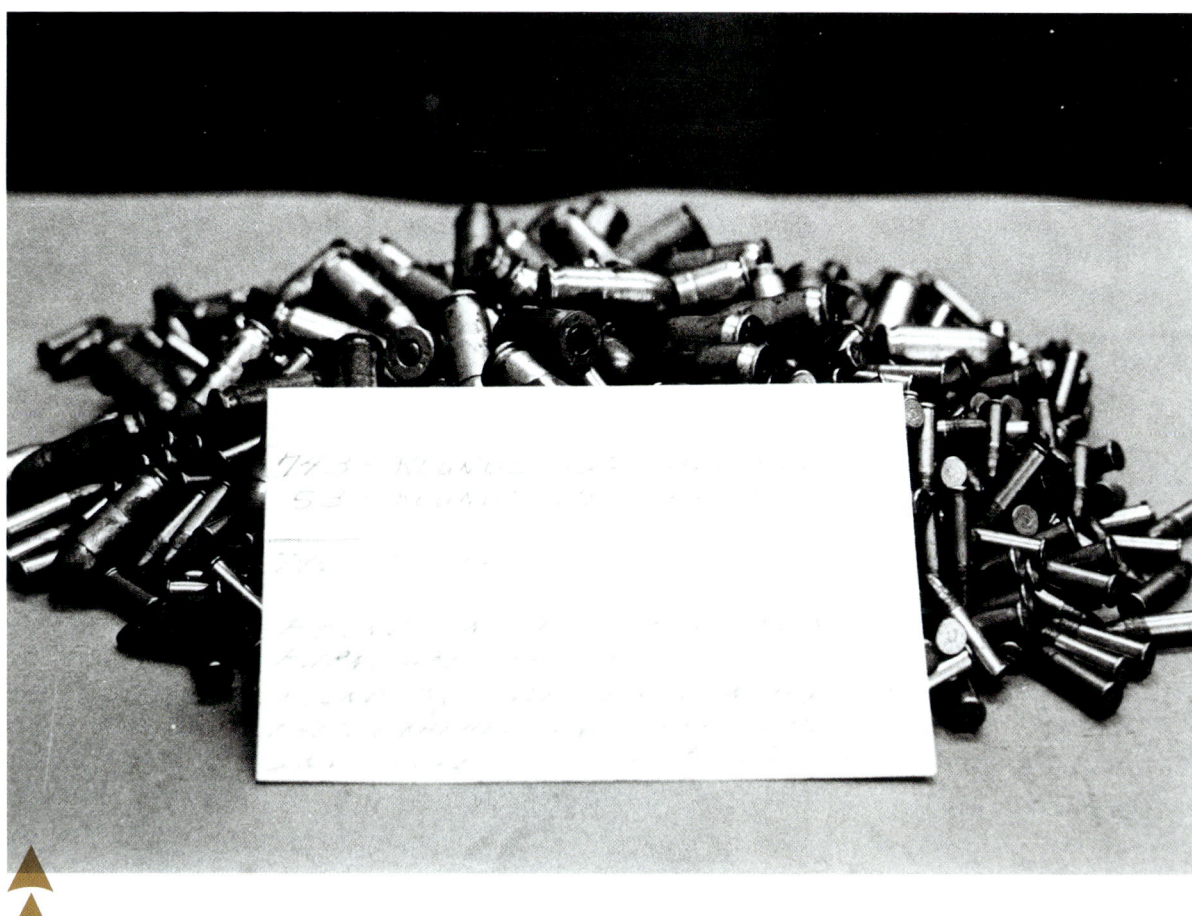

Warden Wyrick recovered 743 rounds of .22 caliber ammo and 53 rounds of .45 caliber ammo, all found in the MSP furniture factory, on May 21, 1975. There was a great deal of unrest and violence at MSP during that time. Lieutenant Harold Atkinson had been stabbed 69 times just a few months prior. His body was stuffed under a bunk in Housing Unit 2/F & G Hall, cell 296. Several firearms and other dangerous items were also recovered following the ammo recovery seen here.

◀◀ A double-bladed axe that was found under an ice chest on the main yard at MSP. The head of the weapon can be unscrewed from the handle to make it easier to hide. Overall length is 19"; the blade is 8" long and 2½" wide.

◀◀ A hacking weapon made from a piece of heavy steel inserted into a pipe handle. A slot was cut into the handle so the blade plate could be slipped into it for added strength. The entire piece was then expertly welded together on both sides. Overall length is 12¾". Blade width is 3¾" and blade length is just under 7".

◀◀ Another axe with a blade that can be unscrewed, similar to the one at top.

◀◀ Here, a blade was inserted between two pieces of oak, and the three pieces were bolted together. The blade is heavy and sharp, and the ends of the bolts were ground off so the nuts would not loosen. The oak handle of this weapon is not as sturdy as those made of steel. Overall length is 15¼". Blade is 8¼" long and 4" wide.

◀◀ A crudely manufactured weapon. The blade is small compared to the other examples. It is only 1" wide and has been spot welded to the heavy-gauge steel handle. The blade is 6" long and the overall length of the weapon is 19¼". Black tape was wrapped around the handle.

Chris Hollaway photos.

An example of how easily a weapon can be concealed. The cribbage board was made at MSP from scraps of oak wood. The board is hollow and the end can be removed. The knife was concealed inside. *Chris Hollaway photo.*

An oak shelf approximately 5' long and 2' wide was found in Housing Unit 4/A Hall. A hollow space had been cut into the shelf on the bottom edge. The shelf had been mounted on a cell wall for several years with a towel draped over the edge. It went undetected for a long period of time. The knife was found inside the cavity. *Chris Hollaway photo.*

This lipstick tube had a knife blade embedded into it. The blade would retract when the tube was rotated. To some, a lipstick tube found in a men's prison might seem odd; however, attempts to smuggle contraband into the prison know no limits.

Three improvised weapons. The top one is made from a modified chisel; length is 4½". The middle weapon is made from heavy-gauge wire; length is 8". The bottom weapon is made for slashing. It is a standard toothbrush with a razor blade attached to the melted plastic; length is 6¾". *Chris Hollaway photo.*

The small steel hammer at lower left was skillfully welded together; a piece of steel bar was used for the head. The remaining weapons were all made from pieces of steel located within the prison. During the late 1960s and early 1970s several attempts were made to racially integrate the MSP. Weapons of the type shown were found and removed by the hundreds. Integration was finally accomplished in the 1970s but not before significant violence erupted in the prison. *Chris Hollaway photo.*

Shoes are often used to hide contraband ranging from weapons to narcotics. This hollow heel was used for concealing drugs.

A knife manufactured commercially to resemble a hairbrush. Contraband such as this innocuous nylon object poses an extreme risk because metal detectors cannot sense it.

The two items seen at right are examples of homemade "stingers," or immersion heaters, used by inmates to heat water for coffee, tea, and so on. Beverage heaters can be legally purchased by Missouri prison offenders; however, many are made illegally. Such items pose an extreme threat to personal and institutional safety because of the potential for shock or fire. Electrical cords would be attached to the homemade gadgets and then plugged into an electrical outlet. Sometimes bare wires are inserted into outlets, which is an extreme hazard.

This piece of pipe is a homemade flashlight used in an escape attempt in the 1970s. Note the small bulb at the end.

A silver pen-type knife where the blade folds into the handle; a knife that looks like a comb when the blade is concealed in the black case; and a lipstick tube with a razor-edge blade concealed inside. These weapons were made for the commercial market. All were found at MSP by alert staff.

Chris Hollaway photos.

Many offenders use talent and skill for illicit purposes. This walnut and cedar stool was made in the furniture factory. Its construction would not have been authorized, although hundreds of furniture items were made and found their way into cell houses.

The maker of this stool cleverly constructed a hollow seat. Without careful inspection that warranted taking the seat apart, the compartment would go unnoticed.

This type of construction is considered "nuisance contraband," but the hidden weapons take the item to a much higher level of concern. The weapons are dangerous contraband and possessing them could result in administrative segregation time, prosecution or both. *Chris Hollaway photos.*

The author had a student in the MSP school in the early 1970s who had this hollowed-out book with a knife inside. The title of the book, ironically enough, was *Murder in a Hurry*. The author became suspicious because the student, who could barely read and write, carried the book to class every day. The author took the inmate by surprise, took the book, and found the knife inside. It was made from a screwdriver. *Julie Woodman photos.*

A unique tattoo device that has been skillfully assembled by using a small motor, various clamps, an electrical cord, a converted tool to hold the tattooing needle, and metal braces bent to accommodate the brass arm by attaching it to the motor. Chris Hollaway photo.

Nuisance contraband is best described as an object that has been altered or is used for something other than its intended purpose. A stack of newspapers and magazines in a prison cell may be nuisance contraband, depending on established institutional rules regulating the amounts of such items. Unlike dangerous contraband, items labeled as being a nuisance generally do not pose a direct threat to the safety and security of prison staff and others. Chewing gum, altered postage stamps, a hollow book, counterfeit canteen coupons, and tattooing devices may all be classified as nuisance contraband. As with dangerous contraband, prison staff must be alert in detecting items that constitute nuisance contraband. A hollow book may contain a weapon, whereby it becomes a component of dangerous contraband. Images of such items are presented on the following pages.

Contraband: Nuisance

Homemade ropes used in unsuccessful escape attempts. Note the two braided ropes, the darker one of denim material. The small white cord in the center is made of braided nylon. The piece of rope at right is toilet paper that was braided to the extent that it could strangle someone. Ropes of dental floss have also been recovered at MSP.

Escapes and attempted escapes are a nightmare for prison officials, but are exciting to the public. Many ask how many escapes have occurred since MSP opened in 1836. The answer is unknown. There were far more escapes from the prison in the "good old days" than there have been in recent times.

The last escape attempt at MSP occurred in 2002. The last successful escape from MSP was in 1986 by Larry Miller, who has yet to be apprehended.

In a 2002 escape attempt, three inmates hid in the prison ice plant, where they worked. Inside a tool room, they made a false wall that concealed an area beneath a stairwell. The inmates stored various provisions over a period of weeks in anticipation that the prison population would soon be moved to the new prison. Due to a reduction in staff, personnel had been removed from the area making it easier for the three to go undetected as they initiated their plan. Staff would come to the location and find them present for the institutional count. Once the staff was gone, the three would continue their plan.

Two elements caused the plot to fail: The three thought the MSP population was going to move in 2002, but the move did not take place until 2004, and one of the three individuals became paranoid. They decided to eliminate the third inmate, fearing he would snitch on them or rat out their plot. They killed him in the ice plant. It took almost two days of intense effort to find them inside their stairwell hideout. They were found and convicted. *Julie Woodman photo.*

A coat lining with sewn-in pockets used to conceal contraband procured for use in an elaborate 1980s MSP escape plot. The liner was worn inside the coat of inmate Elmer "Junior" Herron. He was sent to MSP from the Fulton State Mental Hospital following his involvement in the death of a staff person.

Although Herron put on the appearance of not being mentally stable, he was actually a very cunning man. While working around the prison mowing grass and doing odd jobs, he wore the coat, all throughout the year. He would steal various items needed by men who planned to escape over the main perimeter wall. This photo shows some of the items that Herron managed to steal. Among the recovered items were gasoline, tools, and batteries. *Mark S. Schreiber photo.*

A number of items recovered at MSP that were to be used in a major escape attempt from the prison in the 1980s. These items were found behind a false wall in the inmate law library.

The steel wool at left was being used to build an explosive device that included a compressor and fertilizer. The fertilizer was hidden in the large can with a false top, at left. Fire extinguishers were converted into flamethrowers. The stolen gasoline was to be used in them. The battery packs (right foreground) were from film packs and were to be used to detonate the explosive device, planned as a diversion.

Other recovered items included weapons, a crossbow, homemade hard hats, and tool belts. Several tire inner tubes were also recovered along with homemade ropes. The inner tubes were to help the escapees float down the Missouri River. *Mark S. Schreiber photo.*

A unique cross made from handcuff keys soldered together. The inmate who had the item brought it with him into the prison. A routine search of the new inmate when he was admitted revealed the item. *Chris Hollaway photo.*

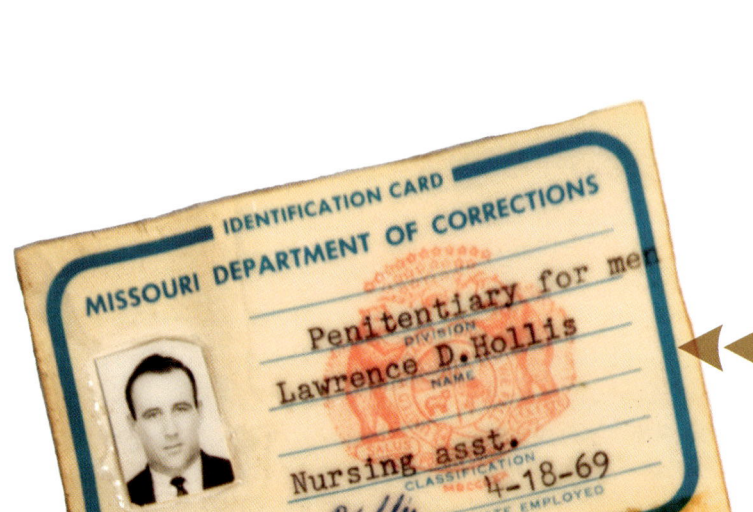

Shown here is a Missouri Department of Corrections employee identification card issued by MSP. The only problem with this I.D. is the photo shown is actually that of an MSP inmate and well-known escape artist. The information shown on the face of the card is also false. This is just one of many games that convicts play. *Chris Hollaway photo.*

A device for spreading the bars of cell windows and doors. It was placed between the bars, with each end against a bar, and a large pipe wrench from the prison plumbing shop would be used to turn the nut at the top end. When done with an even pressure at a slow rate, the bars could be forced wide enough apart to allow an inmate to slip through.

This item was recovered in a mop room of Housing Unit 4/A Hall. During the 2000 filming of *The Big House: Jefferson City* (a History Channel program), an old convict approached the author and stated, "You know that old bar spreader found in A Hall? It'll be an antique when we move to the new prison." When the author asked the old con why he made the statement, he said, "Because we won't have bars on the windows and doors at the new joint." He was correct. *Chris Hollaway photo.*

Innumerable small contraband items were recovered at various times and places at the old Missouri State Penitentiary. The majority of them—including tension bars, jury-rigged keys, lock-picks, and lock-slip devices— were for defeating locks. The author used all of the items shown to train jail and police officers around Missouri.

The three flat, dark objects are pieces of hacksaw blades carelessly left behind by a construction crew.

Pieces of metal from Bic lighters were often made into handcuff keys.

This modified root beer can was used to conceal numerous items of contraband, including narcotics. Prison inmates were using such stash-cans long before they became available for sale on the open market.

Chris Hollaway photos.

More devices for opening locks at MSP. The small object at bottom left was a homemade handcuff key. Prisoners have the patience and the knowledge to defeat any system devised. *Chris Hollaway photo.*

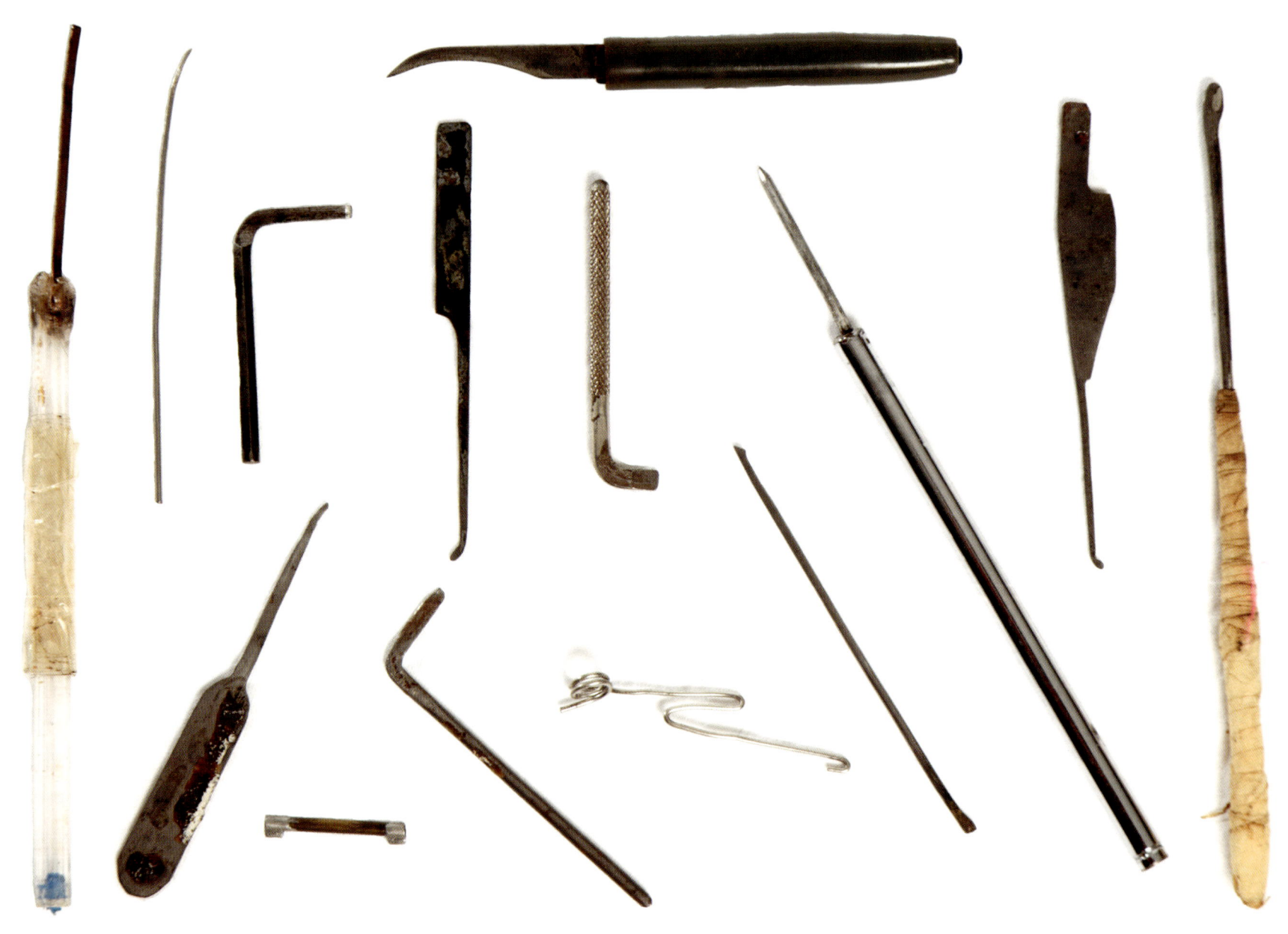

This bar of soap was in plain view, located on a shelf in an inmate's cell in Housing Unit 3/B Hall. Upon closer examination it was discovered that the end of the package was open. The bar of soap contained two .22 caliber shells concealed in the side. A zip gun for the shells was later recovered.

Toothpaste tubes are often used to conceal contraband in prisons. The one shown here was used as a crude pipe for smoking marijuana. Holes were punched into the tube where the two faces are pictured and marijuana was placed over the holes and lit. The prisoner would suck on the open end of the tube, which would draw like a pipe. When not in use, the tube would be blown up to look like it was filled, and toothpaste would be put around the open end to make it look as if it was being used for its original purpose.

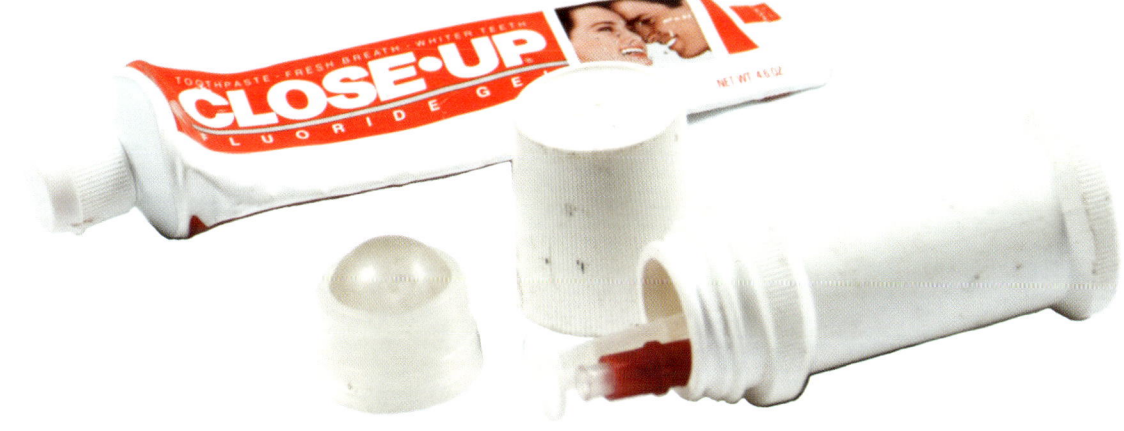

This hollow shaving brush contained two homemade handcuff keys. The key with red paint was made from a tobacco tin.

This plastic roll-on deodorant container had a syringe outfit concealed inside.

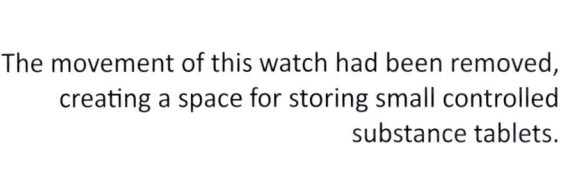

The movement of this watch had been removed, creating a space for storing small controlled substance tablets.

Chris Hollaway and Julie Woodman photos.

Two crudely constructed tattooing devices. Small motors were used, and tape held the pieces together. The top device was wrapped with masking tape, and the shaft was made from a plastic pen. Strapping tape is used on the lower device, and the shaft arm is made of wood. Both devices are missing the needles, which were removed to protect staff from puncture wounds. Tape was also used on such devices to muffle the sounds of the motors. *Chris Hollaway photo.*

Many inmates possess an ingenious creative ability. The tattoo device at the top has a tip made from a ballpoint pen. Another tattoo device, at far left, was made from a small motor, electrical tape, a ballpoint pen, and part of a toothbrush handle. The other items include a small battery pack, a lighter, pen parts, and wire. *Chris Hollaway photo.*

More paraphernalia for prison tattoo work. These were concealed inside a small box. Note the bottle of ink and the small motors that were removed from appliances and rigged to operate the tattoo needle shown at the right. *Chris Hollaway photo.*

A stash of marijuana was found concealed in a hollowed-out book. Staff recovered the contraband in the MSP law library in 1980. *Mark S. Schreiber photo.*

Controlled substances found concealed inside Magic Marker pens at MSP, circa 1981. The prison value of the illegal substances was around $5,000. *Mark S. Schreiber photo.*

Examples of both commercially made and prison-made items used for ingesting controlled substances. At top, a thin straw and piece of plastic tubing were joined together so an inmate could drink a soft drink containing drugs through a mesh screen in the visiting room. Also seen here are syringes, pipes, and coke spoons.

At bottom right, a homemade cooker, used for dissolving a narcotic to a liquid form so it could be mainlined with a needle or hype outfit.

At bottom left, a small brass torch converted into a marijuana pipe.

The author has seen inmates shoot controlled substances into just about every location on the human body: under the tongue, between the toes, and into genital areas. A favorite location is in tattoos, where needle or track marks are difficult to detect. *Chris Hollaway photo.*

This rather large bulldog-style pipe has a replacement stem made of oak.

In most prisons smoking has been a favorite pastime or privilege granted for good behavior or work. The pipes pictured here, however, were not used for conventional tobacco.

This pipe was made from various fittings for smoking marijuana.

A marijuana pipe made from a small piece of walnut scavenged from the MSP furniture factory.

These three small pipes were also used for pot. Note the creative use of discarded bones to construct the bottom two.

Chris Hollaway photos.

The items on this page illustrate the many variations of how wire can be crafted into roach clips for smoking marijuana. Thirteen of these items were made by MSP inmates. The small silver coke spoon at top left was not made at MSP, and the two alligator clips were smuggled into the prison.

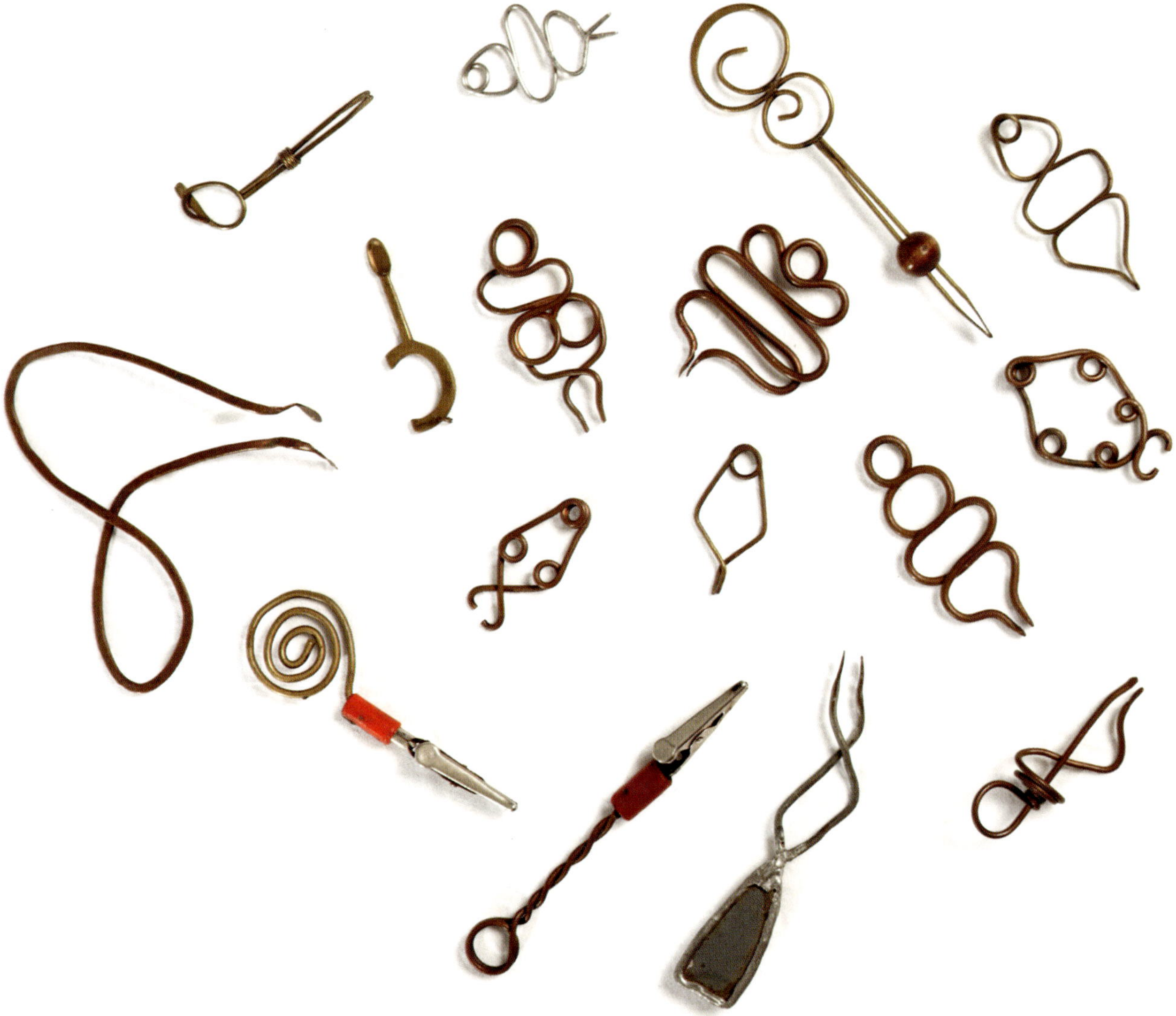

Chris Hollaway photos.

The top rim is damaged, but this sinister-looking bong (water pipe) is unique in its construction. It was made from cardboard, plastic, paper, and glue. The glue had been mixed with wood particles to form the pipe. The interior was lined with a metal soft-drink can.

A miniature, fully functioning, handmade lathe. Although admirable in its way, this and similar items pose a risk for electrical shock or fire in a prison environment. This artifact was loaned by Peter Oetting, a former fire captain (JCFD) and safety manager for the Missouri Department of Corrections. *Chris Hollaway photo.*

Another remarkable creation is this crude but functional electric fan constructed and used by an offender in Housing Unit 4/A Hall. This is one of the author's favorite prison pieces.

This book was in the possession of an offender who learned how to defeat the electronic locking devices in one of the main MSP housing units. The contents of the book are beyond the ability of the author to comprehend. The inmate who possessed it had at one time made gunpowder inside the prison, testing it on a day when thunderstorms shook the facility.

Subject matter of books must be carefully scrutinized by prison staff to avoid problems. In addition to the content, a book's physical properties are considered. Hardback books can be easily used to hide contraband. Meanwhile, it has become increasingly difficult for prison administrators to censor publications because of legal roadblocks. The general rule for censoring a book or publication is that it must be shown to have an adverse effect on the safety and security of an institution.

The item at bottom is a homemade electrical outlet. Note the wood block. Such items are serious safety issues in prisons. *Chris Hollaway photo.*

A short memorandum drafted by MSP Deputy Warden Tom M. Scott on August 15, 1933. It is addressed to Dan M. Carr, secretary to the Penal Board, and advises that a counterfeit 50 cent piece had been discovered inside the institution.

At the bottom of the picture are two 50 cent pieces (tokens). The one on the left is an original token; the one on the right is counterfeit. Notice that the edges of the counterfeit coin are uneven. *Julie Woodman photo.*

At the old Missouri State Penitentiary, if an offender was observed with what looked like newspapers under his shirt or jacket, staff needed to be concerned. Newspapers, magazines, cardboard, and similar materials would be placed under clothing to serve as protection from a knife. This stab vest was made from heavy canvas and has both front and back sections. The straps would go over the shoulders, and the vest would be secured with ties. Heavy material would be placed inside the front and back sections to provide protection. This and several similar vests were recovered at the prison. *Chris Hollaway photo.*

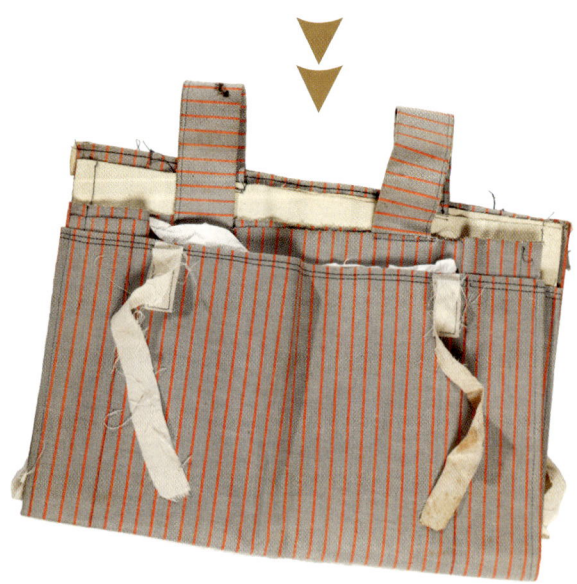

Hundreds of gambling devices have been made and recovered at MSP over the years. At one time, open gambling was allowed in the prison for two days of the year. As strange as it may seem, those two days were the Fourth of July and Christmas! Many inmates, just like people on the outside, will bet and gamble on almost anything. Note the card deck at left that has been hollowed out. The small die at right was made of wood. A variety of substances from clay to metal have been used to make prison dice. Note that one of the red dice has a hole drilled in it. Many pairs of loaded dice have been found at the old prison. If inmate players caught an opponent using loaded dice he might not be around for the next game. *Chris Hollaway photo.*

One of the author's most prized prison mementos is this set of playing cards and poker chips made entirely of leather. Each item is handmade and hand painted. This assortment of cards and chips was handcrafted by MSP master leather artist Gary Reynolds.

The author's research had found that nineteenth century inmates at MSP would create their own card decks and poker chips from leather. They would steal leather from the prison tannery, shoe factories, or the saddle tree factory. Paint was obtained from the prison wagon factory and carefully applied on each card and chip.

Reynolds's masterful reproduction of the old leather decks is outstanding. *Julie Woodman photo.*

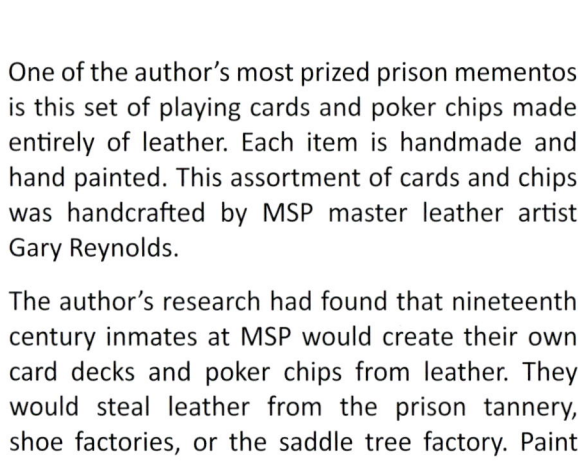

This entire deck, including a full set of chips, was handmade by Reynolds in 2003. The card deck and chips fit into a leather case. Reynolds, serving a term of life plus 50 years, was greatly admired for his talent as a leather worker and wood carver. He died in prison in 2009. *Julie Woodman photo.*

"The Laundry" by Jonathan Humfleet, reflects the reality of prison life. In this work, Humfleet was influenced by Pablo Picasso, father of Cubism, and by Missouri artist Thomas Hart Benton, a founder of the Regionalist School, American Scene Painting Movement of the 1930s. Oil on canvas, 19¾" x 24". Stephen Brooks photo.

In the early 1970s the author was an officer and art instructor at the Missouri State Penitentiary where he developed an appreciation for the artistic talent exhibited by many offenders. Samuel N. Reese was the first prison artist with whom the author worked. Reese was profiled in a *Life* magazine article about prison artists. Prisons are filled with talented artists, some never realizing they had talent until they were incarcerated. MSP was no exception. The men used a variety of mediums and materials, scraps of paper, cardboard, wood, leather, pieces of scrap board, canvas and even toilet paper to create their work of art. Kool Aid and other liquids have been used as coloring agents. Subjects ranged from copies of classical works to original creations depicting prison life. Some ask why offenders should be allowed to create. Art is a form that allows us to express ourselves in a meaningful manner. Although many of the artists at MSP and the new Jefferson City Correctional Center may never leave prison, perhaps through art they can discover the humanity that should exist in every person. The author has an extensive collection of MSP prison art ranging from simple sketches to works in oil, pen, and ink, and carvings in leather and wood. A sampling of these works are presented here.

Art: Paintings to Carvings

These plaster salt-and-pepper shakers are said to have been made behind the walls around the 1940s and 1950s. The salt shaker was no doubt the convict with the smile, and the one with the frown would hold the pepper. These shakers each have "Souvenir of Missouri Penitentiary" stamped on the back. Cork stoppers are in the bottoms. Another pair examined by the author had the date 1951 written on them. John Eidson stated that he remembered salt-and-pepper shakers much like these, but he couldn't remember exactly what they looked like. *Julie Woodman photos.*

This collection of folk art cannot fully illustrate the many beautiful ornaments and decorations crafted by talented and creative inmates. The author has seen everything from toy dump trucks to a detailed fireplace, complete with fireplace tools, all made of cardboard and paper.

The items were displayed by the men of the ITC (Intensive Therapeutic Community) at MSP and later JCCC.

Because no metal was allowed, all the items, from ornate paper chains to fake Christmas tree lights, were constructed of paper, cardboard, and recycled Christmas cards. Once used, the items were destroyed because of a lack of storage space and because they would be a fire hazard. These are small items that were spared from the wastebasket.

At top left, a small wishing-well photo holder. The handle on the well actually turns to raise and lower a bucket on the inside. The item was made by inmate Floyd Newberry, whom the author has known for over 30 years. It was made from folded cigarette liners.

Top row, middle: a small vase containing two flowers constructed of brown paper. The foil rocking chair to its right was also made to hold a small photograph. Inmate Newberry made these items, as well as the Dutch wooden shoes made of foil, seen below the rocking chair. The ornaments in the middle and bottom of the photograph were designed to hang on a full-size paper Christmas tree. *Chris Hollaway photo.*

◀◀ A delicate mobile of origami geese. Talented offenders often make elaborate items from found materials to decorate their cells or to help pass the time. Origami is the traditional Japanese art of folding paper. *Chris Hollaway photo.*

Bugs and Daffy seem to be enjoying a game of pool in this humorous piece of prison art, though no doubt they will argue at some point in the game. Note the badly peeling paint on the steel cell walls. The image located in Housing Unit 2/F & G Hall, cell 56, has almost disappeared. *Stephen Brooks photo.*

Inspired by the U. S. dollar bill, the eye and the pyramid flanked by two palm trees stand watch over an inmate's cell. Above the all-seeing eye is a light socket. In front of the painting is a shelf. Paint and plaster peel from the cell walls at left and right. Note the prison bars located in the middle of the pyramid. The painting was in Housing Unit 3/B & C Hall, cell 114. *Stephen Brooks photo.*

One inmate painted his cell black. A lightning bolt zigzags across the wall, and the skull and crossbones have been painted blue to contrast with the black. At the new JCCC it is a violation of rules for an offender to paint the cell walls. The paint used at the old prison came from State Surplus Property, and making use of it kept the men occupied.

This particular inmate artist obtained the paint from one of the prison shops where he or a friend was assigned. Nude paintings did appear on cell walls at one time, but they were later prohibited, and a violation would be written if compliance was not met. The location of this artwork was in Housing Unit 2/F & G Hall, cell 210. *Stephen Brooks photo.*

A peaceful Native American scene graces a cell. In this tasteful, rather impressionistic painting, all seems well in the mist of a cool early morning with earth and sky blending together while smoke gently rises from within the tepee and an eagle circles overhead. The earth tones of the painted cell complement the scene and even the mattress in the lower foreground. The painting has greatly deteriorated since 2004. Note the peeling plaster. *Stephen Brooks photo.*

Another painting showing the harmony between earth, sky, and water. Shelves are at upper right. *Stephen Brooks photo.*

A portion of a colorful mural from Housing Unit 2/F & G Hall, cell 124. Art of this type, usually landscapes, was done in various locations, such as the old prison chapel, the staff dining room, offices, and common meeting rooms used for inmate activities. *Stephen Brooks photo.*

An unusual piece of prison folk art from a cell in Housing Unit 4/A Hall. The metal tabletop is a checkerboard painted with markers. Markers were prohibited, as the ink was often used in illegal prison tattooing. *Stephen Brooks photo.*

Two of six similar images painted on a cell wall by an inmate who was fond of Harley-Davidson motorcycles. He even painted the Harley logo on the cell wall (not shown). Skulls are often incorporated into art. Another common theme is the Grim Reaper. This work was in Housing Unit 2/F & G Hall, cell 68. *Stephen Brooks photo.*

This unusual paint scheme was in Housing Unit 4/A Hall. The inmate in this cell had other objects attached to the wall where the two oval areas are located. *Stephen Brooks photo.*

These delicate items were all created from toilet paper. The author gave them to the Missouri State Museum so they would not be destroyed. The hummingbird, dragonfly, and spider are incredibly detailed. The bouquet of roses at right was tinted with Kool-Aid. *Stephen Brooks photo. Courtesy Missouri State Museum.*

More toilet paper art. A heart is at the bottom with strands of barbed wire wrapped around it. Roses are delicately positioned on top of the heart and wire. *Stephen Brooks photo. Courtesy Missouri State Museum.*

Prison craftsmanship with a bit of humor. This model biplane was found at Potosi Correctional Center, Mineral Point, Missouri. It had been left in a common area of the maximum-security facility. The craftsman who made the object never came forward; however, an old MSP inmate who was transferred to Potosi was suspected of having made the unique and ingenious model.

It was constructed of cardboard and paper, then painted and stained. The wheels are cardboard and the struts for them are made from Bic ballpoint pens. Wooden ice cream spoons are used for a propeller. The two cockpits have small seats and plastic window visors that are barely visible in the photograph. When the small control sticks in each cockpit are moved, the wing and tail flaps move.

The top wing of the plane reads "Delo Airways." Paul Delo was a lieutenant at MSP, where he served with the author. Delo, now deceased, became the first warden at the Potosi Correctional Center. *Chris Hollaway photo.*

Former MSP inmate Isaiah Jackson completed this painting in 1987. The large panel makes a strong statement regarding American society. Jackson even included his own self-portrait, at the lower left center in the inmate identification card just above the image of Martin Luther King Jr. The MSP watchtower and searchlights are located by the Statue of Liberty in the upper section. The masterful work depicts the demons Jackson faced. The more one studies it, the more one sees.

Jackson completed several other works, and upon his release from prison, he took his works with him, including this painting. He died of natural causes in the St. Louis area. After the move to the new correctional center (JCCC), the author was contacted by Linda Schroeder of Project COPE (program that helps inmates reenter society). She indicated that Jackson's works had gone into private hands and that this painting was the only one left. She asked if it was wanted for the future MSP museum. The work was offered by the author to the Missouri State Museum, but it lacked sufficient storage space. The work is currently stored at another location. Although it deals with difficult subjects, the work is significant and should, by all means, be preserved. *Stephen Brooks photo.*

A photograph cannot do justice to the beauty and craftsmanship of this work. It is a wood carving on pine measuring 54" x 6". It was designed and crafted by inmate Gary Reynolds as a gift from the JCCC staff to the author who retired on April 1, 2010. Reynolds worked on the carving for over a year.

The other inmate artists and staff in the engraving department kept it hidden so the author would not see it during frequent visits to the department. In fact, whenever he made an inspection visit, Bonnie Seaman, his administrative assistant, called ahead to say, "the deputy warden is on his way, so hide the carving."

The work is in great detail and depicts in chronological sequence the author's career in criminal justice. Starting at the left of the panel are the keys to Housing Unit 4/A Hall, which was his first assignment in 1968. Next is Housing Unit 1/H Hall, where he was a zone lieutenant. Portraits of the author are carved in the center; the one at left is from a Civil War reenactment, and the one on the right is from a photo in the *Official State of Missouri Manual*.

The tombstone monuments at the right reflect his involvement in cemetery history and preservation. Next to the tombstones are inmate artists Reynolds (bent over) and Jonathan Humfleet. Both are working in the Hawthorn School, where the author helped establish an art program. Next are the gates to Columbia College, where he received a master's degree and later served as an adjunct professor. The author's Cole County Deputy Sheriff badge is seen at right, along with a bald eagle and the new JCCC, where he served as the first deputy warden of operations after leaving MSP in 2004. The last item, a rocking chair with his pet English bulldog underneath, is a symbol of retirement.

When this masterpiece was presented to the author, he was speechless and overwhelmed. Sadly, Gary Reynolds, master carver, died shortly before the painting on the carving was completed. Before his death, he asked the other men to make sure the work was finished, and they carried out his instructions. The piece will always be cherished by the author. It is signed on the back. *Chris Hollaway photo.*

In this artwork, Gary Reynolds, an MSP offender, depicted Housing Unit 1/H Hall in leather. This structure was built between 1904 and 1906 and was designed by the architects who designed the old City Hall in St. Louis. Reynolds completed this work in 2003, shortly before the old prison closed. It measures 18" x 30¾". *Stephen Brooks photo.*

Housing Unit 4/A Hall, carved in leather by Gary Reynolds. This piece measures 16"x 23¾" framed and is signed in the lower right corner and dated 2002. Reynolds intended to complete a leather picture of Housing Unit 3/B & C, but he died before he could accomplish it. *Stephen Brooks photo.*

A miniature settee, table, and chairs that were made in the Sullivan Saddle Tree Factory at MSP, about 1910 to 1918, for the foreman of the factory, John Tritsch. Tritsch was the great grandfather of the author's wife.

They are made of birds-eye maple, and no nails or glue were used; each piece was crafted from a single block of wood. Height is approximately 4".
Chris Hollaway photo.

A birdhouse depicting Housing Unit 4/A Hall at MSP, which opened circa 1868. The birdhouse was made in January 2003 by "M.X.C.," an inmate at the Northeast Correctional Center. This birdhouse will never see a real bird! Dimensions are 15" x 9" x 8" high. Superintendent/Warden Larry C. Rowley of NECC gave it to the author. *Chris Hollaway photo.*

Quality workmanship is clearly visible in this miniature coffin made from walnut procured from the furniture factory at MSP. Length is approximately 6". *Courtesy of Peter Oetting. Chris Hollaway photo.*

This beautiful and uniquely styled masterpiece by the late inmate artist Gary R. Reynolds is the only Missouri state seal he carved. He told the author that he just wanted to see if he could do one. Twenty inches in diameter, the seal is carved out of Missouri white oak which is hard and difficult to carve. The grizzly bears and center section are of Missouri walnut. Reynolds gave dimension to the seal by having the grizzly bears stand alone in the center.

Unseen in this photo is the area behind the bears where Reynolds carved other Missouri symbols, including the Missouri mule, a bluebird, grapes, and oak leaves. Incorporated into the design is the Missouri state tree, the dogwood. The edges of the seal are carved, which is most unusual.

Reynolds signed the work on the back. He told the author that he planned to do only one seal, and he wanted the author to purchase it. He also included his original drawings for the seal. The author purchased the seal through Missouri Vocational Enterprises. There have been several talented carvers of Missouri state seals at MSP, but none have matched the creative genius of Reynolds. *Chris Hollaway photo.*

Miniature guitar made at the prison for John G. Tritsch. It has several missing pieces but still shows the skill of the inmate artisan. *Chris Hollaway photo.*

This gavel was made at MSP around 1900 and belonged to John G. Tritsch. *Chris Hollaway photo.*

This jewelry box shown was given to the author by a close friend and former neighbor, Louise Hansen. The item was crafted for her by an MSP offender who worked as a computer programmer. He was later convicted of first-degree murder in the homicide of two Jefferson City residents and was executed for the crimes. *Chris Hollaway photo.*

This rare jewelry box was made for Captain Leroy C. Casey by an unknown inmate. It is made like a safe, with a handcrafted locking device in the door. The man who made this had knowledge of how a safe worked. Height is 14". *Chris Hollaway photo.*

The same jewelry box with the door closed. Note the safe handle and dial. *Courtesy Mr. and Mrs. Allen L. Sartain.*

Ozark Smoking Tobacco was manufactured by the MSP Prison Industries. The tobacco burned so fast it would singe the eyebrows. Relics like this are difficult to find because the product was used or thrown away. Courtesy Bob and Barb Van Ark. Stephen Brooks photo.

Miscellaneous items from the author's collection are presented in the final pages of this book. Several smoking items are shown on page 136. The prison-made ashtray is especially unique as the bottom of it can be removed to reveal a hollow space. When it was recovered, several dollars in currency was discovered hidden in this space. In the Missouri Prison System, currency is contraband. Hundreds of miscellaneous items are scattered throughout the country. Perhaps many will reappear as relics of historical interest and will someday be placed in a museum where they can tell the story of one of the influential institutions of our country, the Missouri State Penitentiary. The lessons from the past create a future where many prisons, such as MSP, will just be a chapter of the past.

Miscellaneous Artifacts

Smoking and chewing have always been enjoyed by inmates. Tobacco products used in the old MSP included Ozark Chewing Tobacco, which was made inside the prison. Ozark Smoking Tobacco came in a drawstring cloth pouch with cigarette papers included. Prison-made smoking tobacco burned too rapidly to provide much smoking pleasure. Only men who could not afford other tobacco products used it in later years.

Brown's Mule and Days O Work were two commercial types of chew available. Commercial cigarettes, "tailor made" in prison slang, were sold in the inmate canteen in later years. Commercially made tobacco products were always preferred by the prison population and served as a means of barter or for paying debts.

Cigarettes were often illegally brought into the prison. In one instance, a prison-raised cat called Old Mike was fitted with small cloth saddlebags tied around his middle. Cigarettes and other contraband items were placed in the bags. Old Mike would carry the items into isolation cell areas, where he went to be fed. It took some time for staff to determine how the items were being delivered to the inmates in the old segregation unit.

The ashtrays below are some of many produced from scrap wood by creative men at MSP. Note the ornate walnut-grained cigar holder at the middle. Such items have little monetary value but are historical. *Julie Woodman photos.*

A homemade token and coupon box used at MSP. The tokens came in denominations ranging from five cents to one dollar.

Tokens, and later coupons, were used by inmates to purchase goods from the prison canteen. MSP tokens were first issued during the 1920s, with the coupons being issued later and printed in small booklets. This metal box was used to collect the tokens and coupons at the prison canteen until the 1970s. *Chris Hollaway photo.*

MSP canteen tokens used during the administrations of Wardens John S. Crawford (1925–1929) and J. M. Sanders (1933–1937). The octagonal five-cent token was used when William Kruse was prison secretary, during the administration of Warden S. T. Nix (1929–1932). Tokens were made in denominations of five, ten, twenty-five, and fifty cents. There were supposedly one-dollar tokens, too, but the author has not seen one from MSP. Ironically, the rarest of the tokens shown here are the ones that are blank or in the process of being counterfeited. *Chris Hollaway and Julie Woodman photos.*

Following the use of tokens as currency at MSP, coupons were issued. Official U.S. currency was and continues to be prohibited inside Missouri prisons. Coupon books were issued to the men and paid for with money from their prison accounts. On average, a twentieth-century inmate made $7.50 per month, though an inmate with special skills could earn substantially more.

Most inmates received money from family members and friends on the outside. The money could not be mailed directly to the inmate but could be sent to the prison financial officer and deposited to the inmate's account. Goods available through the inmate canteen would be purchased with the trade coupons. Records were kept of all transactions.

Inmates caught with coupon books that were not issued to them, or had been altered in any manner, were in violation of institutional rules.

Inmates were also not allowed to have more than a specified number of coupon books in their possession. Those with too many coupon books or canteen items usually were operating an illegal store, selling or trading unauthorized items at inflated rates to other inmates. Such practices were not uncommon and often led to serious consequences when disputes erupted between the men.

Here is a unique example of misguided inmate talent. The tan coupon book, numbered 25251, is legal. Note the watermark on the yellow coupons below. The coupons at the bottom with the numbers 20248 are counterfeit. Approximately $2,500 worth of these counterfeit coupons were either passed at the MSP canteen or recovered. The inmate who made them worked in the engraving section of the license plate factory in the old prison.

Once coupons had been spent at the prison canteen, civilian staff was directed to remove and destroy the outside covers. But sometimes careless staff did not handle the process correctly, and inmate canteen workers obtained the empty covers.

The counterfeit coupons were then stapled into the empty covers. The coupons were distributed throughout the institution and passed at the canteen during peak spending days. Deputy Warden Bill Armontrout, Sergeant Don Wells of the Missouri State Highway Patrol, and the author worked the case. *Julie Woodman photo.*

Food-service items from the MSP dining room. At one time, a wooden board was used to serve prisoners held in the dungeon cells located under Housing Unit 4/A Hall. The oldest cups on this page are the ones at right.

During the 1970s and 1980s, hard plastic cups were introduced. They were light tan or blue-green. During the 1960s through the 1970s, eating utensils consisted of metal butter knives and forks which were often converted into lethal weapons.

In the early days, inmate food consisted of little more than beans, hash, cornbread, and coffee or water. On Christmas and the Fourth of July, the inmates were provided higher-quality food.

The small bowl at left has no markings. The cup second from left is marked "Wear-Ever #212 Aluminum." The cup at center was used with the bowl and plate. It is marked "Crusader" with a crusader emblem engraved on it along with "L&G Mfg. Co." The cup second from right is marked INFA type 430. The plate is stamped "State of Missouri." *Chris Hollaway photo.*

Items from the old MSP food service department. Such artifacts are often overlooked as having no historical value. As a result, they become difficult to locate. The stainless steel pitcher was standard at the prison for many years. More than one fight behind the walls involved pitchers being thrown by unruly men in the dining room. This pitcher was recovered by the author while making a walk-through of the facility several months after it closed in 2004. Use of these pitchers had been mostly discontinued several years prior to the prison closing. This pitcher is on exhibit at the new prison.

The metal serving tray was previously used by the U.S. Navy. It is marked on the bottom and was used at MSP in the late 1940s and early 1950s. This type of tray was probably in use at the time of the 1954 prison riot. John D. Eidson, son of Warden Ralph N. Eidson, gave the tray to the author, saying that he remembered the tray being used when his father served as warden. *Chris Hollaway photo.*

Early MSP uniforms like this were made of wool or muslin to make the inmate as miserable as possible. This was the norm for the punitive Auburn System, under which the Missouri State Penitentiary operated for over 100 years.

The uniform below is not original, as only part of an original one is known to exist. Zebra-striped uniforms like this were worn at MSP until about 1912. After 1912 some were worn by inmates in the punishment unit.

The uniform pictured here was made for the author in the 1970s by an old inmate, Raymond P. Patrick. He was an excellent tailor—and escape artist. Patrick made this uniform and one for Deputy Warden Bill Armontrout. The uniforms were worn in Christmas parades.

During the 1940s through the 1970s, inmates wore uniforms of blue, green, or gray. The green uniforms of the 1960s and 1970s had a black stripe running down each pant leg. The green cap had a stiff bill. Inmates with trustee status wore whites with a black stripe down each pant leg.

Chris Hollaway photo.

◄◄ This shoe last— a metal form for making shoes— was used in a shoe factory that operated at MSP in the early 1900s. It was later owned by the John G. Tritsch family. Tritsch worked as a factory foreman in the prison during the early years of the twentieth century. *Chris Hollaway photo.*

This small hammer was used in the Sullivan Saddle Tree Factory and belonged to foreman John G. Tritsch. *Chris Hollaway photo.* ►►

John G. Tritsch collected many artifacts from MSP. From left is a small hammer used for saddle tree construction, a two-piece glue pot with ladle used for making saddle trees and for shoe manufacture, tongs used to handle hot coals, and square nails.

The large ice tongs at right were made at the prison. They are crude in construction, but managed blocks of ice well. They were used at Tritsch's Café located in the Millbottom District on West Main Street, across from the old railroad roundhouse.

Mr. Tritsch started the café after leaving the saddle tree factory. Tragically, he was shot and killed in the café during an armed robbery in November 1923. The two men who shot him were sentenced to life behind the same walls that Tritsch had worked within.

His son, Robert, continued to operate the café through the 1950s. *Chris Hollaway photo.*

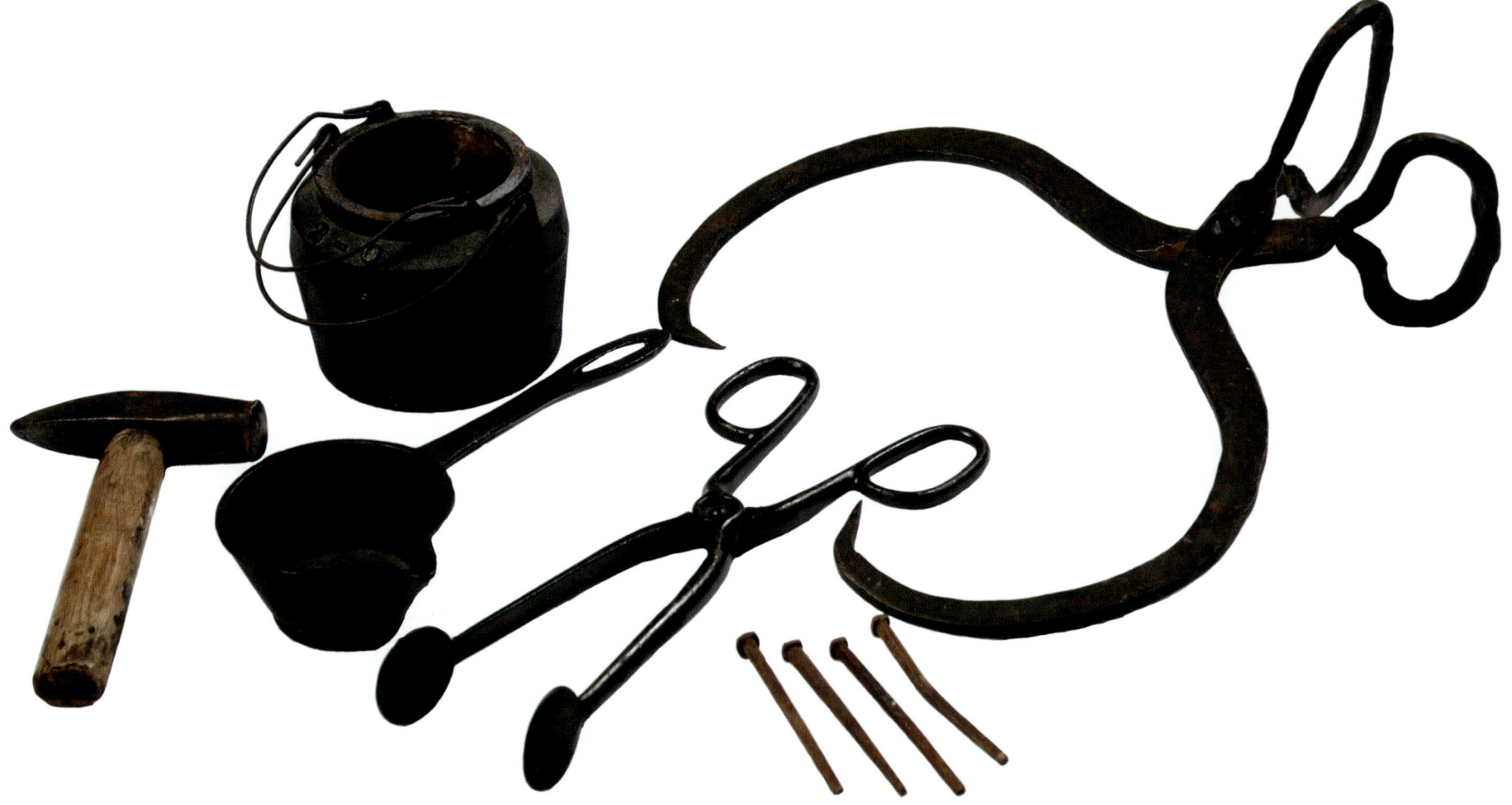

What would a prison be if it didn't manufacture license plates? This is the steel die for the 1936 Missouri license plate. After the September 2004 move from the old MSP to the new location six miles away at JCCC, the license plate operation continued. This item was given to the author by Jefferson City antique dealer Tom Benke. *Chris Hollaway photo.*

A relic from the old prison, one of three cameras that were used to take inmate identification photos until the late 1940s. The homemade I.D. plate at left was used to identify the inmate, who would hold it in front of himself as the photo was taken. The numbers on the plate could be changed by sliding them on or off. A Model 2 Eastman View camera manufactured by Eastman Kodak Company, it takes 4" x 5" and 5" x 7" photos and has a Wollensak lens with a sliding carriage. Thousands of photos were taken by this camera and others. *Courtesy Warden Dave Dormire MSP/JCCC. Chris Hollaway and Lloyd Grotjan photos.*

The author expresses his sincere appreciation to the many individuals and organizations who assisted in the publication of this book. If someone was omitted, it was without intent.

PHOTOGRAPHS

Chris Hollaway, Stephen Brooks, Julie Woodman, Lloyd Grotjan and Aaron Reed

Unless noted otherwise, artifacts and photographs in this book are the property of the author.

The author expresses his appreciation to the Discover Jefferson City Foundation for its support of this project, and especially to Steven Picker and Sarah Alsager.

Special thanks to Charles Brzuchalski for his great support and assistance in researching architectural elements for this project.
Special thanks to Louise Schreiber who spent countless hours editing the drafts for this publication.

CONTRIBUTING ORGANIZATIONS

Jefferson City Convention and Visitors Bureau
Jefferson City Correctional Center
Missouri Department of Corrections
Missouri Office of Administration, Division of Facilities Management
Missouri Secretary of State
Missouri State Archives
Missouri State Highway Patrol
Missouri State Museum
Missouri State Penitentiary Redevelopment Commission

Associated Press
Chicago Tribune
Jefferson City News Tribune
State Historical Society of Missouri
St. Louis Post-Dispatch
St. Louis Globe-Democrat
United Press International
Walsworth Publishing Company, Dennis Paalhar
Wears Creek Yacht Club
Western Missouri Historical Manuscript Collection

CONTRIBUTORS

Laura Adams
Sarah Alsager
Bill M. Armontrout
Tom Benke
Bill Berry
Bob Blosser
Roger Boyd
Trenton Boyd
Louis Bredeman*
Michelle Brooks
Phyllis Brooks
Stephen Brooks
Charles Brzuchalski
Richard G. Corser
Hugh Dallas*
Shelby Debler
Mrs. Albert DeBroeck
Dave Dormire
Jim Dyke
Edgar Eagan*
John D. Eidson
Ralph N. Eidson*
Phillip Farris
Charles Ferrell
Bill Green
Michael Groose
Ed Hanauer Jr.
Harvey L. Harris
Kathern S. Herigon
Gail Hughes
Jonathan Humfleet
Kate Keil
Joe Kroeger*
Mrs. Raul (Rose) Lazzarini
George Lombardi
Mike Malone
H. D. Marshall
Ray Miller
Mrs. E. V. Nash
Richard Nash*
Floyd Newberry
James F. McHenry*
Mark Noe
Clifford Oetting
Peter Oetting
Steven Picker
Bernard J. Poiry*
Bob Priddy
Fred Rackers *
Gary Reynolds*
Larry C. Rowley
Mr. and Mrs. Allen Sartain
Elaine Schollmeyer
Debbie F. Schreiber
Kent S. Schreiber
Bonnie Seaman
Lyndall Shive
Laurie Stout
John L. Sullivan Jr.
Anthony Susnick
Harold R. Swenson*
Tom E. Tetrick
Mr. and Mrs. Bob Van Ark
Phillip E. Vance
Fr. Clarence P. Wheeler
Charles Wilson
Zeal Wright*
Donald Wyrick*
Susanne Young
Tim Young

* Deceased

Grateful acknowledgement is made to these individuals whose generous gifts of stories, expertise, time, and support have made possible the publication of this book.

As if to defy the wrecking ball, the old MSP Administration Building casts a golden glow on the evening of October 9, 2007. Its final chapter remains to be written. Mark Schreiber photo.